Developing Students' Coding Skills
An Implementation Guide for Grade 6-12 Educators

Kevin M. Steele, Ed.S.

International Center
for Education

If you can't fly, then run,
if you can't run, then walk,
if you can't walk, then crawl,
but whatever you do,
you have to keep moving forward

~Martin Luther King, Jr.

Table of Contents

To my wife, Lauren, a true warrior!

To my children Johanna, Olivia, and Andrew everything is possible!

To my mom and dad for the love and support in all the things I do!

Special Thanks to One of My Greatest Friends, Kristin Love Webster, for the cover design. It is always nice to have chosen family!

Kevin M. Steele, Ed.S.

Founder/CEO
International Center for Education
kevin@icecollaborate.org

icecollaborate.org

Dear Colleagues,

Coding is the "New Literacy." Our students are growing up in a quickly changing digital world and coding is a language they'll need to know. Coding is not just for the computer class or the after-school club, it is an integral part of the curriculum and can be integrated into every subject. Coding promotes problem solving, critical thinking, creativity, communication, collaboration, reasoning, spatial awareness, sequencing, and so much more. It is STEM (Science, Technology, Engineering, and Math) education at its best!

The introduction of teaching coding has been gaining interest and generating buzz the last few years. This book is designed to put you in the coding seat and work the projects that you can implement with ease and very little preparation. The book is written in a handbook form for you to use what you can and leave the rest. Some may find it as a means of implementing the curriculum and others may find experiences of educators that make their teaching with technology more efficient.

I have designed this book for all levels of technology users, from the tech timid to the tech savvy, to teach coding. Coding can and should be taught at every grade level. There is an abundance of resources, mostly free, that grow daily and I will help you sort through them to find the best. We will look at ways to design lessons and projects to infuse coding into our everyday curricula. We will discuss the research and real-world application and dive deeply into the extension lessons for coding. Through this book, we will be working through many of the projects and you will possess not only the inspiration, but projects, lessons and ideas. There is not just one way to teach coding. I will help you get started and give you the tools and resources you need to move your students forward.

The book promises to be filled with practical activities, ideas, tips and resources that will empower you to infuse coding and reveal the magic behind the screens!

Sincerely,

Kevin M. Steele, Ed.S.

About the Author

Kevin Steele was born and raised in the suburbs of Chicago. He has travelled extensively for both business and pleasure. This continues to be one of his favorite hobbies.

He currently lives in Northwest Indiana with his wife Lauren. Lauren is also a passionate educator having won several awards for her influence in K-4 reading intervention. Together, they have two beautiful daughters and one amazing son.

Kevin's professional interests involve technology integration to support the whole learner. He believes students are at the core of our profession and we must leverage our knowledge of current research, best practices, curriculum, technology and many other variables to provide access to the best educational experience possible for every child.

Kevin's professional career has included both teaching and training environments for learners from Kindergarten up to adult. A bulk of his career was spent in the middle and high school classrooms teaching technology, science and social studies.

Kevin is currently the Training & Distance Learning Consultant in the Office of Information Technology at Valparaiso University in Valparaiso, Indiana. In this position, he manages the instructional technologies to connect learners and faculty throughout the world in online settings (both synchronous and asynchronous) in many programs throughout the university.

In March 2012, Kevin was in Gurgoan, India to present at the International Conference on Strategy, Innovation and Technology at Ansal University. He has presented at many national conferences throughout the United States and Canada to audiences that leave refreshed and invigorated after spending the time with him. His energy, enthusiasm and passion for education are infectious.

Kevin Steele is available for national and international conference presentations, consultations and teacher training sessions.

Visit Kevin on the web for more resources, tutorials and all things teaching and learning!

kevinmsteele.com

Online Resources

Resources will certainly change as the book goes to print, so in order to address that and keep the resources up to date, a resource page is available that will be updated as time moves along. By joining the resource page, you will have access to a community of educators that are also embarking on the same journey into coding at all levels. We are using Schoology to cultivate these resources. Please follow the instructions below to access the page.

    a. Go to Schoology.com
    b. Create an instructor account and fill out the required information.
    c. Once you have signed up, go to COURSES menu.
    d. Click on JOIN in the bottom of the fly out menu.
    e. Type in the following code:

V6GQ5-M3GRP

If you are already a Schoology user, please sign in and go to Courses > Join. This will prompt you for the code above.

Pre-Reading Self-Assessment

DIRECTIONS: Please fill out the following self-assessment prior to working through the book. We will repeat this process after you have worked the book for you to measure your progress and the quality of what you have learned. Be honest, don't over-interpret questions...go with your gut!

Rate your current understanding of coding (the practice of, not the teaching of coding).
   a. Mark Zuckerberg ain't got nuttin' on me!
   b. I have coded a few things and they seem to work just fine. So, I am fairly comfortable.
   c. No formal experience, just tinkering around. I can do a few things.
   d. I can type my garage door code...does that count?

List three goals that you have for attending today's workshop. This is what you want to bring back with you. You have to have these things to call the workshop a success!

   1. _____

   2. _____

   3. _____

Without looking forward in the handbook, what is your understanding of coding or code?

What types of resources do you use to find, cultivate and store your technology tools?

What is your coding class vision?

How do you currently organize your class content for the students to access?

Chapter 1

GETTING STARTED

"Do what you can,
with what you have,
where you are."

~Theodore Roosevelt

The basis of this chapter is to get started in a technology-rich learning environment. Most educators find that many of the suggestions, tips, or strategies are easily adapted to any tech-rich environment. Please feel free to adapt, change and fit these ideas to your school/district culture, students' needs and parents' expectations. There is not a "one-size fits all" approach to teaching in any subject. We must be careful to state that this is true of coding and technology education, too.

Mom: Honey, please go to the market and buy 1 gallon of milk. If they have eggs, buy 6.

Son: *(comes home with 6 gallons of milk)*

Mom: *What possessed you to buy 6 gallons of milk?*

Son: *BECAUSE THEY HAD EGGS!*

Computers are literal, simple and fast. The above dialogue illustrates the logic in which computers understand instructions we give them. This is why we find them so frustrating!

Introduction to Coding

A History & Definition

Computer code is what makes all our devices work. The trouble with defining it comes in trying to make it seem less technical and more understandable. Sure, we could give examples, but that sometimes introduces new terminology that muddies the water. To keep this simple, we will look at the idea of "code" as it evolves through history.

The word first shows up in relation to computers in the Association of Computer Machinery databases in 1954, but is getting reference in 1946 from Professor Howard H. Aiken of Harvard University (Hopper, 1952).

We can look back even further into the timeline to 1801, to the invention of the mechanical, automated loom. The loom worked using programmable punch cards that controlled the operation of the loom. The loom did not use electricity, but human interaction was required for power. The difference was the pattern of the output was controlled by what the loom read on the card as it passed in the overhead bins. This eliminated many errors in the construction of the textile.

As time went on, the sense of programming and coding was left to mathematicians. Many of the machines were not programmable in a digital sense until World War II. During the war, the Colossus machine was the first programmable, electronic digital computer that was designed to break and read encrypted German messages.

From that point, machines kept getting bigger, stronger and more complicated. The era of code was upon us; but only for the highly skilled mathematicians. It wasn't until the 1980's when coding skills made their way into education through BASIC programming.

Today the definition is expansive, but my favorite comes from urbandictionary.com (don't share that site with students...although they already know about it; you could get fired.), which explains it as, "Basically, telling your computer to do stuff using a programming language. As long as the computer understands the code, it will execute the command blindly."

In all seriousness, the word code or coding is substituted for programming. Merriam-Webster defines it as a set of instructions for a computer. When we look at the definition it is simple and understated. However, it is true. All you are writing is a set of instructions; but in a way that the computer can execute the commands. It's really a series of "If...Then..." statements.

Another interesting find was the use of the word in the ACM databases surged around 1990 through 2010. Since then, the articles being published seem to have dropped off. Is it because the use of the phrase code is falling out of favor? Or, that the coding phenomenon is on a pendulum switch? Of course not, we are only half way through the decade. We will surpass the previous decade in articles published.

The word is really referencing mathematical functions for telling the computer how to perform a specific set of tasks. As it evolves, the details of "code" become more complex. We see that not every code is the same. Some computers need something "coded" differently to understand it. The computer languages or programming languages do vary; but the understanding of the basic ideas will apply throughout.

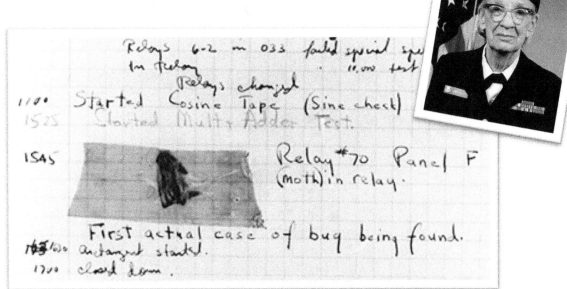

Figure 1 - Grace Hopper discovered the first computer bug. Quite literally a moth stuck in the punch cards. It was saved and taped into the notes, thus coining the term "bug" when referring to errors in the code.

Establishing Classroom Rules

As we have been taught since the very beginning of our study of teaching and learning, establishing classroom rules is extremely important to a successful school year. I would argue that rules are important; but many of us miss the boat on setting up learning rules and focus on behavior rules. To me, those are procedures and they are taught. My class rules focus on learning. I find that when these are stated, behavior comes along for the ride. The following are my established rules and what they actually mean to me and the students in my room.

1. Always code as if the guy who ends up maintaining your code will be a violent psychopath who knows where you live.

When I am working with students individually or in small groups, talk a lot about the "violent psychopath." This is really a metaphor to explain to students the need to be concise, efficient and accurate with syntax. When I see an area for improvement in their work I ask, "What would the psychopath say about this?" Imagine the look on an administrator's face when that gets asked during an evaluation or when the students begin to discuss the psychopath in front of them. Words cannot express my joy in watching an uncomfortable administrator trying to figure out why this discussion is so commonplace in my classroom.

2. Never fear creativity!

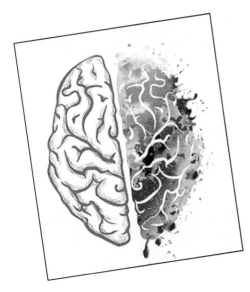

I always want to encourage my students to go above and beyond or to explore a new avenue for their skills. They just need to talk through the exodus from my plan with me. Throughout the discussion, I am testing their theory with the underlying question, "Does this meet or exceed the learning goals?" I look for reasons to say "YES." The fact is, I don't care how they learn it, or how they show me they learned it; but that they can do both. If they fail to reach their goal, they learn about failure. In that case, their grade is based on reflection; which we do together.

3.   All assignments are learning opportunities!

Students do not have to do any of
the assignments they don't
choose. However, when they
don't have the skills they were
taught in those activities, they are
redirected back to those. They
quickly learn that success resides
in the learning opportunities.
Projects and assessment points
are not optional, however!

4.   Failure does not exist…only missing semicolons!

This is a very important rule. Students must learn frustration
and failure coping mechanisms when working with code.
Students are quick to blame themselves. In fact, female
students will blame themselves first. They will tend to use
possessives in explaining it to you, "MY code is not working," or
"I don't get this." Male students on the other hand leave out
the possessives as though the code is outside of them. Use the
undo button on their screen and you will see they have
attempted. In my class, you are not allowed to blame yourself.
You can blame the computer, the code or the psychopath; but
not yourself. (A great video in Segment 4 folder on Schoology
by Reshma Soujani provides further explanation.)

I also keep coding board games in the classroom and allow
them to do homework from other classes at points. I
remember when I was coding at a previous job, I had points
where I had to put it down and busy myself with other things.
Frustration was too great! It was in those "other" times that
the solutions would reveal themselves. This is what I want my
students to be able to do, too.

5.   Have fun! Talk! Share! Find your passion (or your future spouse)!

I try to encourage an office-like workspace. Students should feel free to collaborate, create together and find their own path. That is what real-life is all about. I also explain this one a bit more to them. In my own junior year of high school, I was assigned a group. In it was this girl I had known about, but not really talked to before, and we were made partners for our project. Well...20+ years later, we are married with three children. Fate (and a school project) brought us together...and she was (and still is) really cute, too!

Management Techniques for Tech Integration Lessons

Training Students to Work in A Tech-Rich Environment

Students can easily get off task. How do we stop that from becoming a major issue through lessons where they are online? Off task behavior is one of the major issues that I hear time and time again from educators. Here are some simple practices that may the management of a technology-rich classroom.

1. Decide on your "Acceptable Use Policy" for classroom technology and post them so they can be easily read in passing when students come in to work for the day. These are the class rules that they can be expected to be accountable for while using the technology in the classroom. These may include the following:

   - Devices will be flipped and flat when somebody is addressing the whole class.
   - Ask 3 before me.
   - Need to check something? Do it...then get straight back to work!
   - Know your lab manager and be extra kind to them.
   - If it's broken, please report it!
   - Help others with your mouth, not their mouse.

2. Use a lab manager for your extraneous tasks. Train a student to refill the printer, connect devices to the Wi-Fi, direct students to applicable tutorials, etc. When you find something that disrupts you from working with students, train your lab managers in each period how to complete the tasks. The bonus is that they will show the other students how to do these tasks and your students will be less reliant on you and more self-sufficient as the year goes on.

3. Have non-tech solutions for students who make a habit of being off-task. Simply modify on the fly. Here are some examples:

Tech Task	Non-Tech Alternative
Taking electronic notes	Have a place ready to go for students to grab paper and a pen so you can point.
Building code for a program	Students can map it out and illustrate logic by hand until they can earn back their device.
Designing a user interface for a new program/app	Start with the storyboarding or wireframes drawn out.

4. Think about the layout of the room. The more screens the teacher can see at any given time or place in the room...the more on task behavior you will observe. I always prefer a perimeter of seats on the outside of the room where students have to turn their seats to face inward. When working on their computers, the face the outside walls of the room. Two U-shape configurations will also work quite nicely. Of course, there are some great furniture options that really enhance the tech environment. (I know...budgets!!!)

5. You are free to move about the cabin! The more you move, the better it will be for the students on task behavior. Without knowing where you might be next, they tend to stay on task. Raise their level of concern!

6. Make sure all their learning resources are organized and easily located. Using an online LMS will assist with this. Details located on page 17 entitled, Learning Management Systems (LMS)

The above list is not an exhaustive list of management techniques for all classroom; but more can be found at the following addresses:

For Further Exploration Online

5 Tips for Surviving Tech Integration in the Classroom: http://goo.gl/prj2SK
From my personal blog on tech integration. These are the lessons I learned from my students. These tips have helped me keep my sanity!

Intervention Central: http://goo.gl/1ZBYZl
Great for school-wide and classroom interventions to increase on-task behaviors in any classroom.

Edudemic: http://goo.gl/2oWC4Y
Creative hacks for increasing student productivity is the title of the article; but it offers great advice and setup for new teachers or experienced teachers needing a refresher.

Implementation Plan Worksheet

1. Observe each student typing a paragraph.

   a. How many are using the correct hand placement?

   b. How many are using the "hunt & peck" method?

   c. How many can type at an average speed or higher?

   Students above grade 6 need to know how to type. This will be the first differentiation for those that can type versus those that cannot. Even if keyboarding is taught at a younger age, finger dexterity changes as the student's hands grow. It may need to be revisited. Resources can be found at the following:

      i. EduTyping.com (Paid – but well worth it!)
      ii. Typingclub.com
      iii. Typing.com
      iv. keybr.com

   > STRATEGY TIP: If typing is required, we were able to break this into our homeroom activities. We setup a rotation where I, as the technology teacher, would teach typing for 6 weeks to each homeroom. We had 6 teachers on a team. The students were broken into 5 homerooms. This gave one teacher a free period each rotation. I got my free rotation at the end of the school year (evil genius).

2. Assess the availability of technology and select your materials accordingly.

   How many computers (desktops/laptops/tablets) do you have for students to use on a daily basis (or on coding lesson days)?

   While there are a variety of activities that can be done without technology, if you are teaching a course in coding, the best possible scenario for long-term learning is to conduct the class in a computer lab or a 1:1 environment. Students find a great deal of value when they can see their finished products working (or better yet, not working). It excites and motivates them.

   If you are lacking resources, you can always pair this down into an afterschool activity, a small term course, a hybrid math/coding course or use it as 20% time in a course. This will free up computers for the sharing of resources.

3. Assess the dedication of the administration.

    Do your administrators support the teaching of coding?

    Do the other faculty members understand the logic of coding and how it strengthens students' problem-solving skills?

    Some may struggle getting others on board with the concept of teaching coding; but here is a little advice for those that are still information collecting. Of course, you can always host after-school activities, clubs, etc. This is a great place to start to gain some momentum. If you are considering running a course on this topic, be sure that administration understands the concept of coding and how it enhances student learning. If they don't understand coding (in brief), and support it, budget matters and other considerations may be stacked against you. This will only require some time, research, patience and persistence.

4. Gauge student interest and understanding.

    Do your students understand what makes their favorite apps and programs work?

    Do they show interest in making changes and suggesting enhancements to those favorites?

    It is always amazing to have students define what coding and programming is and how it works. They are able to define it; but it is relatively magic to those that have not experienced coding. We always assume that they are so gifted and natural with technology. Some are; but their understanding of the under the hood parts is still a mystery to them.

5. Host an Hour of Code event.

    An event like this should be done each year in a mass effort to get students interested and expose students that wouldn't normally be exposed to coding. The first may be the roughest if students have not been previously exposed. However, the students should run subsequent years' events. Their passions become infectious!

Hour of Code Event
hourofcode.com/us

In order to excite students about coding, consider hosting an Hour of Code event. Whether you are looking to promote your coding classes, or if you are getting started in the introduction of coding to your school, the #hourofcode might be just what you are looking for in an event to get everybody pumped up about coding! You will be in awesome company! The map below illustrates global locations of events so far. Sign up your school and you will be added to the map.

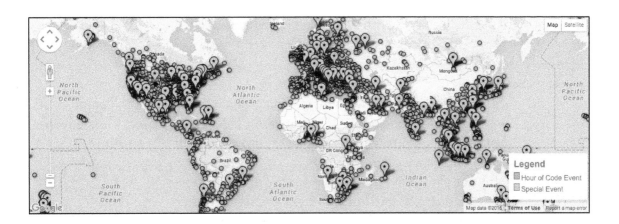

The Hour of Code is a non-profit organization sponsored by several technology companies. They will provide all the resources that you need to host an event of your own. The companies all have a vested interest in assisting educators...it's educating the next generation of coders. Surprisingly, there is a shortage of programmers and coders. Positions at companies are open for anybody with the skills.

Our school put one together and had students in programming classes host workshop events at small tables. The students in coding classes planned their activity they would host at their table. Some stations were teaching Scratch, while others were using Makey Makeys and another table had robot equipment out. The coding students were offered extra points for every friend that attended and wrote their name in for the "invitation" to attend. Students showed up to support friends and actually drew quite a large crowd. The event was a huge success that resulted in the development of cross-curricular courses such as coding and music.

As a side note, our semesters break and finals are placed right in the December period where the Hour of Code events are usually planned. We host ours in the beginning of the spring semester outside the "recommended" timeframes. The Hour of Code police haven't knocked down our door, yet!

The 20% Project

3M started it in the 1950's with their 15% project. The result? Post-its and masking tape! Google is credited for making the 20% project what it is today. They asked their employees to spend 20% of their time at work to work on a pet project...a project that their job description didn't cover. As a result of the 20% project at Google, we now have Gmail, AdSense, and Google News. Innovative ideas and projects are allowed to flourish and/or fail without the bureaucracy of committees and budgets. (Petty, n.d.)

This would be a great way for you to introduce coding to students if time is not set aside for the course, or if resources are sparse and/or shared with other colleagues and students. Why not make this a Monday activity?!?!

Katie Petty has some great rules and more ideas on her blog at: thetechclassroom.com

Rules:
1. You may work alone or with a small group.
   - Decide carefully. If you choose a small group, you will have to compromise with your group and deal with other personalities. If you work alone, you have complete autonomy but you are responsible for the outcome.
   - Is this person a worker or floater?
   - Can I get along with this person for the entire semester?
   - Is this person going to keep on track or distract me?
   - This is not about hanging out with friends, but making something really cool.
2. Choose a project that is new to you and something you wouldn't normally do in another academic class.
   - If you are stuck, do some research on other educational 20% projects and take another look at what Google has done.
3. You must produce a product.
4. Write up a proposal and pitch it to the rest of the class that includes a purpose, audience, timeline, and resources you will need to complete the project. You will present your pitch in a "science-fair"-type poster session in front of other students, teachers, and community members.
5. Choose an adult to be your official mentor. I am an English teacher, I do not have a lot of experience with some of the projects you might choose.
6. Reflect on the process each week on the class wiki or personal blog.
7. If, at any moment, you feel lost, overwhelmed, or uninspired, you must set a meeting with me to find a solution.
8. At the end of the year, you will present your project and reflect on the process in a five-minute TED-style talk.
9. Failure is an option. Simply learning from your mistakes teaches you a lot.

Learning Management Systems (LMS)

Learning management systems will provide your class with a virtual space outside of your classroom walls. An LMS is the foundation of classroom/project management in your coding class. This will be the space that will house all of your classroom resources (calendars, links, learning materials, tutorial videos, etc.) for students to access when class is not in session. Trust me when I say that you and your students will be glad you made this change if you have not already done so. You will save time, cut excuses and your students will be more independent.

There are several to choose from and I have listed a few with some summary information and links. Some are paid, some are enterprise specific and others are free and available to start today. I will, of course, start with my favorites:

Schoology
www.schoology.com
Cost: Free

Enterprise systems are available for a fee and added management. However, it works just fine in the free version.

With Schoology, educators can do things as simple as posting assignments, quizzes and links to additional resources or as sophisticated as conducting online courses, providing one-on-one remediation, or hosting discussions. Videos can be uploaded directly to their servers for playback on many devices.

The User Interface (UI) is very much like Facebook. Students and teachers will already have a start on understanding its setup and training will be limited. Additionally, they have an app in both the Apple and Android Marketplace. The app has recently undergone some really great upgrades to allow grading and class management directly.

Advanced users will be able to manipulate the pages and customize the placement of information. The gradebook is fully integrated and you can grade where the assignment has been placed or directly in the discussion board. One major feature to the discussion board is the ability to filter by user. This feature saves a great deal of time when trying to figure out if a student met all the requirements of the post and responses to others.

Edmodo
www.edmodo.com
Cost: Free

With Edmodo, educators can do things as simple as posting assignments, quizzes and links to additional resources or as sophisticated as conducting online courses, providing one-on-one remediation, or hosting discussions.

The User Interface (UI) is very much like Facebook. Students and teachers will already have a start on understanding its setup and training will be limited.

There are some restrictions to interfacing with your resource library and your ability to control where information can be located. However, the resource library and the ability to multi-post for multiple class sections is a huge time saver.

Blackboard Engage (formerly Edline)
www.edline.com
Cost: Varies—Must be purchased as a school or district

Edline offers individual class web pages where content can be stored. There are size limits to the file sizes, but videos can be embedded using their HTML coding (it's not as hard as it sounds) feature in their rich text editor.

One of the key features of Edline and their add-on gradebooks is that they offer interfacing between your school's Student Information System (SIS) and their system. This can cut down significantly on grade reporting and setup.

Since Blackboard's acquisition, Edline has been receiving many upgrades. Schools seem to enjoy Edline because it can be branded to them using their design features and the interfacing solutions save time on the backend with reporting and management.

Moodle
www.moodle.com
Cost: Free'ish

This is open-sourced software that can be installed on your servers or through Moodle-partners (there's the 'ish part...)

Many schools that I work with love their Moodle sites. However, I will caution that many of these schools have been developing their sites and the features for years and are bit more advanced in their technical understanding.

My experience with Moodle is limited; but I would be remiss if I did not include it since so many schools have experienced success with Moodle's implementation. My limited understanding leads me to believe that this is the most fully customizable and flexible, but it is also not the friendliest with organizations that want to get started today!

Collaborize Classroom
www.collaborizeclassroom.com
Cost: Free

This is a new collaboration space that is available for free to teachers and students. It has some really nice reporting features and topic libraries that are

continuing to grow. The class pages also allow teachers to create flexible groups to work on differentiated problems. Polling questions can be assigned to videos or attachments to assess student understanding. The site also features an app in the Apple store for both students and teachers.

One thing that I liked about this platform was the ability for students to post their work and get peer feedback. They can also break out into groups and work collaboratively from a distance on their project.

Canvas

Cost: Free – purchased version available to schools/districts

Canvas is a product developed by the company Instructure. They are making huge strides in breaking the Blackboard curtain in higher education and have proven themselves within the K12 arena, as well. The user interface is simple and easy to understand for both students and instructors. Teachers and students will spend most of their time in the Courses section of the platform. In the free version, teachers provide their own content and walk their students through the registration process. In the paid version, the IT department can upload students and use data transfer to collect grades. As I collaborate with schools, I am finding that more and more schools are adopting Canvas.

Google Classroom

Cost: Free

Google Classroom has shown a great amount of interest in the marketplace and some very tech savvy teachers are endorsing it via social media and through collaborative events such as conferences and workshops. Why is it at the bottom of my list? It makes the bottom very simply because it is not a learning management solution. It is a great place for you to integrate your Google Drive and other items if you are full Google school. However, it is missing a gradebook, automated grading (in a simple form) and collaborative/discussion posts. Therefore, it makes a great website for your class; but a learning management tool…I am hoping that gets some attention.

Chapter 2

TOOLS TO CODE

"Everyone should know how to program a computer,
because it teaches you how to think!"

~Steve Jobs

The basis of this chapter is to introduce a plethora of resources for you to consider in teaching both yourself and your students to code. Most educators are excited by the opportunity to teach something as engaging as coding; but have so many trepidations about teaching in an area where they, themselves, can be baffled. These are great opportunities for you to model failure, uneasy coping strategies, seeking assistance, working a problem, etc. Do not fear the unknown, embrace it. Don't worry...many of your students are not whiz kids who know more than you on the topic (notice I used the word many...not all!). When it comes to coding, many students appear to be more advanced. They are coding savvy, however most do not understand the logic. That is your main focus in teaching them coding. Teach them to think in a logical, deliberate and concise way.

Introducing Coding

The good news about coding is that there are many options available to us and we can do virtually anything we want. The bad news is that there are so many options available to us and we can do virtually anything we want. The positive becomes the negative when we are new to this idea and we are looking for a place to start. The limit is our own imagination; but predicated by fear of doing something wrong or being outsmarted by our students. Don't worry, they will outsmart you! They always do! Isn't that exactly what we want?

When starting the curriculum, assume that all students are starting at square one. Your more advanced students will identify themselves pretty quickly. Those students that have already been coding often lack the foundation of logic. They have taught themselves how to code by watching others on YouTube and online discussion boards. Many have not actually written code from the beginning; they have simply cut and pasted from online sources and tweaked the code. In such cases, they still need the basics.

To start the curriculum in my courses, I start with basic coding exercises in learning the logic. Many online resources are available for you to use which include the grading, feedback and assistance. Students can work at their own pace. I interject projects into each academic quarter to break up the monotony of the process. We will discuss this further in Chapter 3.

The first place I start is with an offline coding exercises (one is reprinted under the next heading) and offline games. This gives me an idea of how many of my students understand basic vocabulary and logic that goes into the algorithm. For students that need a bit more assistance, I will infuse games. There are some great, offline coding games with online guides to stretch students further.

Offline Games

Certainly not a comprehensive list, but a start. These games are great for remediation, or entertainment for your advanced students. In the initial introduction of coding they are used to reinforce the logical thinking. Later, the games can be used as a strategy for pacing. All games are available on Amazon.com and other online and brick and mortar retailers.

Code Master
By ThinkFun

This is an individual player game that has variations to make the game easy for newbies or challenging for more advanced students.

Code Monkey Island
By Code Monkey Island

This is a spin on *Sorry!* by Hasbro. However, there are a series of cards that require if:else statements, parameters and some function cards. Although, they are disguised as just playing cards. The resource book is the best part of the game going forward. It has online activities that students can complete that teach coding.

Robot Turtles
By ThinkFun

This game is so flexible with level of difficulty. My son, 8, and my daughters, 9 and 13, love playing this one together. It can span ages very well and is all about movement logic and concise process.

Graph Paper Programming Lesson
Adapted from: https://goo.gl/2uVPpA

LESSON OBJECTIVES	TEACHING GUIDE MATERIALS, RESOURCES AND PREP (Print & Video Resources at the link above)
• Experience the difficulty of translating real problems into programs • Differentiate between ideas which may feel clear and yet still be misinterpreted by a computer • Practice communicating ideas through codes and symbols	• Four-by-Fours Activity Worksheet • Graph Paper Programming Assessment • Sheets of 4x4 paper grids for the students to use as practice (These are provided as part of the Four-by-Fours Activity Worksheet, but if you have the students create their own, you can include Common Core Math standard 2.G.2.) • Blank paper or index cards for programs • Markers, pens, or pencils • For the Teacher • Lesson Video • Print out one Four-by-Fours Activity Worksheet for each group • Print one Graph Paper Programming Assessment for each student • Supply each group with several drawing grids, paper, and pens/pencils

GETTING STARTED (15 MIN)

1) Vocabulary
This lesson has two new and important words:

> *Algorithm* - A list of steps that you can follow to finish a task
> *Program* - An algorithm that has been coded into something that can be run by a machine

2) Introduce Graph Paper Programming
In this activity, we are going to guide each other toward making drawings, without letting the other people in our group see the original image.

For this exercise, we will use sheets of 4x4 graph paper. Starting at the upper left-hand corner, we'll guide our teammates' *Automatic Realization Machine* (ARM) with simple instructions. Those instructions include:

• Move One Square Right

- Move One Square Left
- Move One Square Up
- Move One Square Down
- Fill-In Square with color

With one little substitution, we can do this much more easily! Instead of having to write out an entire phrase for each instruction, we can use arrows.

In this instance, the arrow symbols are the "program" code and the words are the "algorithm" piece. This means that we could write the algorithm:
"Move one square right, Move one square right, Fill-in square with color"
and that would correspond to the program:

Using arrows, we can redo the code from the previous image much more easily!

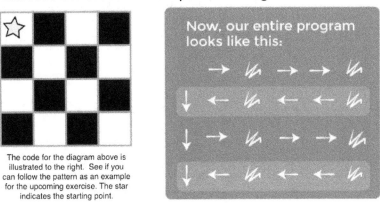

The code for the diagram above is illustrated to the right. See if you can follow the pattern as an example for the upcoming exercise. The star indicates the starting point.

3) Practice Together
Start your class off in the world of programming by drawing or projecting the provided key onto the board.

Select a simple drawing, such as this one to use as an example.

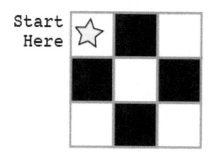

Start
Here

This is a good way to introduce all of the symbols in the key. To begin, fill in the graph for the class -- square by square -- then ask them to help describe what you've just done. First, you can speak the algorithm out loud, then you can turn your verbal instructions into a program.

A sample algorithm:
"Move Right, Fill-In Square, Move Right, Move Down
Fill-In Square, Move Left, Move Left, Fill-In Square
Move Down, Move Right, Fill-In Square, Move Right"

Some of your class may notice that there is an unnecessary step, but hold them off until after the programming stage.

Walk the class through translating the algorithm into the program:

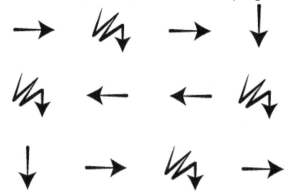

The classroom may be buzzing with suggestions by this point. If the class gets the gist of the exercise, this is a good place to discuss alternate ways of filling out the same grid. If there is still confusion, save that piece for another day and work with another example.

Start
Here

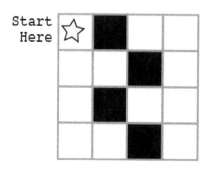

If the class can shout out the algorithm and define the correct symbols to use for each step, they're ready to move on. Depending on your class and their age, you can either try doing a more complicated grid together or skip straight to having them work in groups on their Four-by-Fours Activity Worksheet.

LESSON TIP
Have the class imagine that your arm is an Automatic Realization Machine (ARM). The idea of "algorithms" and "programs" will be brought to life even further if students feel like they're actually in control of your movements.

ACTIVITY: GRAPH PAPER PROGRAMMING (20 MIN)

4) Four-by-Fours Activity Worksheet
- Divide students into pairs.
- Have each pair choose an image from the worksheet.
- Discuss the algorithm to draw that image with partner.
- Convert algorithm into a program using symbols.
- Trade programs with another pair and draw one another's image.
- Choose another image and go again!

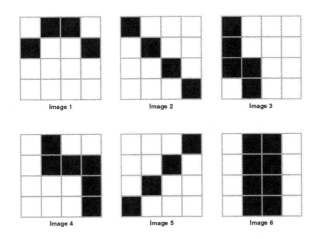

WRAP-UP (5 MIN)

5) Flash Chat: What did we learn?
What did we learn today?
What if we used the same arrows, but replaced "Fill-In Square" with "Lay Brick"? What might we be able to do?
What else could we program if we just changed what the arrows meant?

6) Vocab Shmocab

Which one of these definitions did we learn a word for today?
- "A large tropical parrot with a very long tail and beautiful feathers"
  "A list of steps that you can follow to finish a task"
  "An incredibly stinky flower that blooms only once a year"
- ...and what is the word that we learned?
- Which one of these is the most like a "program"?
      *A shoebox full of pretty rocks
      *Twelve pink flowers in a vase
      *Sheet music for your favorite song
Explain why you chose your answer.

ASSESSMENT (10 MIN)

7) Graph Paper Programming Assessment (Online at link above)

EXTENDED LEARNING
Use the activities at the top link to enhance student learning. They can be used as outside of class activities or other enrichment.
- Better and Better
- Have your class try making up their own images.
- Can they figure out how to program the images that they create?

Name: _____   Date: _____

Graph Paper Programming

Unplugged   Four-by-Fours Activity Worksheet

Choose one of the drawings below to program for a friend. Don't let them see which one you choose!

Write the program on a piece of paper using arrows. Can they recreate your picture?

Use these symbols to write a program that would draw each image.

| → Move One Square Right | ← Move One Square Left | ↑ Move One Square Up | ↓ Move One Square Down | ⟋ Fill-In Square with Color |

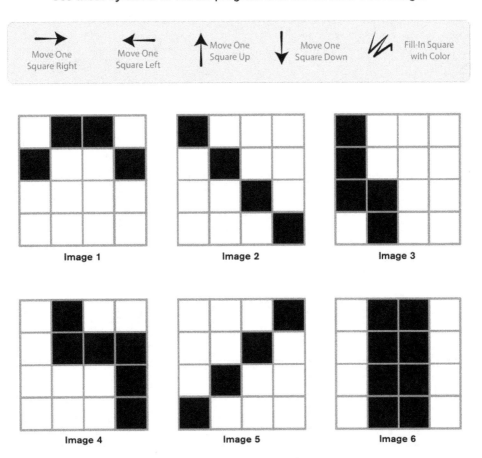

Image 1   Image 2   Image 3

Image 4   Image 5   Image 6

Revision 140830.1a

©Kevin M. Steele, Ed.S.

Connections to Standards (Graph Paper Coding Activity)

ISTE Standards (formerly NETS)
1.b - Create original works as a means of personal or group expression.
1.c - Use models and simulation to explore complex systems and issues.
2.d - Contribute to project teams to solve problems.
4.b - Plan and manage activities to develop a solution or complete a project.
4.d - Use multiple processes and diverse perspectives to explore alternative solutions.
CSTA K-12 Computer Science Standards
CPP.L1:3-04 - Construct a set of statements to be acted out to accomplish a simple task.
CPP.L1:6-05. Construct a program as a set of step-by-step instructions to be acted out.
CT.L1:3-03 - Understand how to arrange information into useful order without using a computer.
CT.L1:6-01 - Understand and use the basic steps in algorithmic problem-solving.
CT.L1:6-02 - Develop a simple understanding of an algorithm using computer-free exercises.
CT.L2-07 - Represent data in a variety of ways: text, sounds, pictures, numbers.
NGSS Science and Engineering Practices
K-2-ETS1-2 - Develop a simple sketch, drawing, or physical model to illustrate how the shape of an object helps it function as needed to solve a given problem.
3-5-ETS1-2 - Generate and compare multiple possible solutions to a problem based on how well each is likely to meet the criteria and constraints of the problem.

Common Core Mathematical Practices
1. Make sense of problems and persevere in solving them.
2. Reason abstractly and quantitatively.
3. Construct viable arguments and critique the reasoning of others.
6. Attend to precision.
7. Look for and make use of structure.
8. Look for and express regularity in repeated reasoning.

Common Core Math Standards
2.G.2 - Partition a rectangle into rows and columns of same-size squares and count to find the total number of them.

Common Core Language Arts Standards
SL.1.1 - Participate in collaborative conversations with diverse partners about grade 1 topics and texts with peers and adults in small and larger groups.
SL.1.2 - Ask and answer questions about key details in a text read aloud or information presented orally or through other media.
L.1.6 - Use words and phrases acquired through conversations, reading and being read to, and responding to texts, including using frequently occurring conjunctions to signal simple relationships.
SL.2.1 - Participate in collaborative conversations with diverse partners about grade 2 topics and texts with peers and adults in small and larger groups.
SL.2.2 - Recount or describe key ideas or details from a text read aloud or information presented orally or through other media.
L.2.6 - Use words and phrases acquired through conversations, reading and being read to, and responding to texts, including using adjectives and adverbs to describe.
SL.3.1 - Engage effectively in a range of collaborative discussions (one-on-one, in groups, and teacher-led) with diverse partners on grade 3 topics and texts, building on others' ideas and expressing their own clearly.
SL.3.3 - Ask and answer questions about information from a speaker, offering appropriate elaboration and detail.
L.3.6 - Acquire and use accurately grade-appropriate conversational, general academic, and domain-specific words and phrases, including those that signal spatial and temporal relationships.

Coding Resources

Scratch

scratch.mit.edu

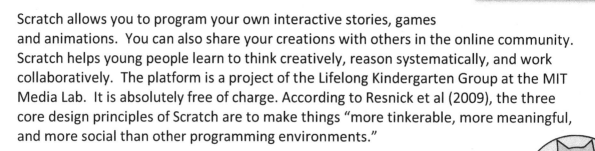

"'Digital fluency' should mean designing, creating, and remixing, not just browsing, chatting, and interacting (Resnick et al, 2009)"

Scratch allows you to program your own interactive stories, games and animations. You can also share your creations with others in the online community. Scratch helps young people learn to think creatively, reason systematically, and work collaboratively. The platform is a project of the Lifelong Kindergarten Group at the MIT Media Lab. It is absolutely free of charge. According to Resnick et al (2009), the three core design principles of Scratch are to make things "more tinkerable, more meaningful, and more social than other programming environments."

This section will only "scratch" (groans) the surface of what the platform can do for you and your students. Their site is a wealth of resources that are more highly visual, interactive and complete than here. This section will be presented more as a "Getting Started Guide" rather than a manual. Much of this information is also found in the Help Section of Scratch. Be sure to refer to the Help Section if something is not as printed in this book.

Scratch has a teacher project book, learner workbook and presentation formats that can be edited for teachers. Visit their page at: https://goo.gl/ErLWlI

Scratch User Interface

The user interface for the Scratch development environment divides the screen into several panes: on the left is the stage and sprite list, in the middle the blocks palette,

and on the right the scripts/costumes/sounds editors. The block palette has code fragments (called "blocks") that can be dragged onto the scripts area to make programs (called projects). To keep the palette from being too big, it is organized into 10 groups of blocks:
Motion, Looks, Sound, Pen, Data, Events, Control, Sensing, Operators, and More Blocks (custom-built blocks and extensions).

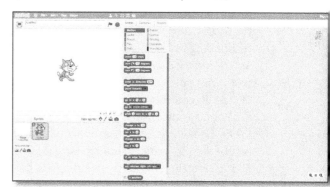

ScratchEd

Launched in July 2009, ScratchEd is an online community where Scratch educators share stories, exchange resources, ask questions, and find people. The site boasts more than 7500 educators from all around the world have joined the community, sharing hundreds of resources and engaging in thousands of discussions. To join the community visit scratched.gse.harvard.edu.

Alice
alice.org

Alice is an innovative 3D programming environment that makes it easy to create an animation for telling a story, playing an interactive game, or a video to share on the web. Alice is a freely available teaching tool designed to be a student's first exposure to object-oriented programming. It allows students to learn fundamental programming concepts in the context of creating animated movies and simple video games. In Alice, 3-D objects (e.g., people, animals, and vehicles) populate a virtual world and students create a program to animate the objects (What is Alice?, n.d.).

In Alice's interactive interface, students drag and drop graphic tiles to create a program, where the instructions correspond to standard statements in a production oriented programming language, such as Java, C++, and C#. Alice allows students to immediately see how their animation programs run, enabling them to easily understand the relationship between the programming statements and the behavior of objects in their animation. By manipulating the objects in their virtual world, students gain experience with all the programming constructs typically taught in an introductory programming course.

Unlike Scratch, Alice is a software platform that must be downloaded on machines. The technical requirements (Dann et al, 2014) are listed below:

Minimum system requirements
- Desktop or laptop computer. Alice runs okay on some netbooks. However, many netbook models are not powerful enough to support 3D graphics animation. We suggest a trial run of a sample Alice 3 program on any netbook being considered for purchase.

- Windows XP, Vista, Windows 7, Mac OSX (Leopard, Snow Leopard, Lion, or Mountain Lion), or Linux

- 1 GB RAM (2 GB or more is recommended)

- VGA graphics card capable of high (32 bit) color and at least 1024x768 resolution (3D video card gives faster performance)

- Two- or three-button mouse is recommended. The touchpad on a laptop may be used. Please note, however, that arranging 3D objects in a virtual world is easier to control with a mouse than with a touchpad.

The Getting Started Guides for this resource are copyrighted and therefore accessible online in the Schoology page for this workshop or at: http://goo.gl/NMPRch

Code.org
code.org

"Launched in 2013, Code.org® is a non-profit dedicated to expanding access to computer science, and increasing participation by women and underrepresented students of color. [Their] vision is that every student in every school should have the opportunity to learn computer science. [They] believe computer science should be part of core curriculum, alongside other courses such as biology, chemistry or algebra (code.org, n.d.)."

The organization has built a full learning platform for both the students and teacher. The entire site is free for use. It includes both opportunities for student learning and professional development for teachers who are new to the computer sciences or need a brush-up or training in coding. They also have a complete repertoire of lessons and lesson plans for you to choose from to match your students' needs.

Code Studio

Code.org's Code Studio has some great introductory lessons for students to get acquainted with the logic of code. It also helps set the stage for upcoming lessons and projects that can be built using code. It starts with the simple block style coding of scratch; but reveals the JavaScript that is being compiled behind the scenes. The full Code Studio can be viewed at studio.code.org. This resource is also posted on the workshop Schoology page.

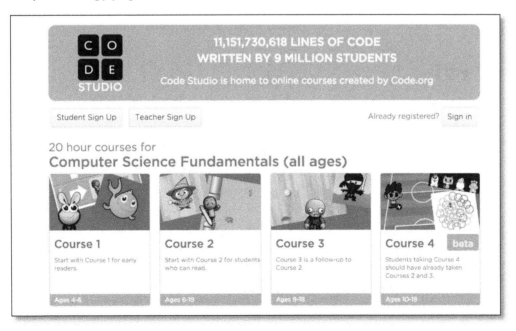

Resources & More Resources

This section is a list of online resources that you can use in the classroom. While there are resources throughout the book; you will find this is a place to find new ideas and inspiration when starting out, or when things feel that they are too routine. This list is also found on my Pinterest board. It will be updated as new things are found! (The book does have a few limitations.)

You can find my Coding Board at:
https://goo.gl/Rorqow

	Teaching Kids to Code **Ideas for parents and teachers**	**A collection of a few tools to work on problem solving and design. The main goals of this site are 1) keep learning fun and 2) focus on scientific thinking through the design process. Below are a few tools in my toolbox at the moment. Let me know what you think!**	**http://goo.gl/GdWcPi**
code jam	**code jam** by Google	Google Code Jam returns for the 13th year as one of the most challenging programming competitions in the world, and we're excited to announce new changes! The contest, which consists of intense algorithmic puzzles held over multiple online rounds, and culminates in an Onsite Final round, is ever-expanding.	https://goo.gl/uamFKL
KHAN ACADEMY	**Khan Academy** Computer Programming Course List	Learn how to program drawings, animations, and games using JavaScript & ProcessingJS, or learn how to create webpages with HTML & CSS. You can share whatever you create, explore what others have created and learn from each other!	https://goo.gl/j2HJK4

	Codecademy	Code Academy is a resource that is better for older kids (pre-teens and teenagers). It is much more advanced than Scratch. It is an online interactive platform that offers free coding classes in programming languages like Python, PHP, JavaScript, and Ruby, HTML and CSS.	https://goo.gl/yNFTfE
	Alice	Free downloadable software that teaches computer programming in a 3-D environment. Kids can create animation, games or videos to share on the web. There's also quite a collection of resources for teachers.	Alice.org
	BitsBox	Monthly subscription service that sends a box of programming challenges for kids, along with lesson guides and other goodies. (Paid $20 to $40/month)	Bitbox.com
	BotLogic	Introduces basic programming concepts by asking players to navigate a series of challenging mazes.	Botlogic.us
	CargoBot	Players learn coding logic in this iPad app by using a string of commands to organize crates with a robotic arm. As levels get more complex, the user must create functions and optimize his limited number of moves to meet the objectives.	http://goo.gl/GuhFDM
	Code.org Studio	Offers free basic and intermediate modules featuring cartoons and characters from Angry Birds to Star Wars and beyond, for use at home or in the classroom. Teachers can access a dashboard to track student progress.	studio.code.org

	CS Unplugged	Here's a nifty trick—learning computer science without a computer! This series of logic exercises uses cups, ping pong balls and post-it notes to teach students the logic behind coding. The site also has videos of each exercise being used in a class.	csunplugged.org
	Karel Coding	Self-paced online programming course that's currently used in schools, programming clubs and at homes. The course includes an optional algorithmic thinking pre- and post-test.	nclab.com/karel
	Move the Turtle	Based on the Logo programming language, this iOS app helps players learn coding logic by guiding a turtle through obstacles to a destination. Players can also use its composer function to create intricate designs.	movetheturtle.com
	Pluralsight	Offers free coding courses for kids on Scratch, HTML, App Inventor, Kodu and Hopscotch	https://goo.gl/GQjz0R
	RoboLogic	Players program a robot's movements on a grid and get it to light up specific squares before they run out of moves. Teaches concepts of functions and nesting.	https://goo.gl/VbOFQw
	Turtle Academy	A collection of short, free lessons using the Logo programming language. Students will learn the basics of programming logic in this browser-based program.	turtleacademy.com

Learn to Code with Visual Blocks

Product	Price
App Inventor for Android This MIT-created platform uses visual blocks to allow students to create apps that can be exported to Android devices. Large library of tutorials that get as advanced as SMS texting and GPS. Requires a Google Account to use.	Free
Hopscotch This free iPad app uses a visual programming language similar to Scratch to help kids learn the basics of programming logic, such as sequencing, loops, variables, functions and conditionals.	Free ($0.99 for in-app purchases)
Scratch 2.0 Created at MIT, Scratch popularized visual blocks as a way of learning programming. But don't let the easy interface and cute graphics fool you-- users can make and share anything from simple animations to fully-fledged games.	Free
SNAP! SNAP!'s visual blocks support higher level computer science concepts like recursion, procedures, and continuations, making it appropriate for even college level intro classes. While it doesn't have the same social functions of Scratch, SNAP! can work with the Nintendo Wiimote and LEGO Mindstorms NXT. Comes with a manual and sample projects and can use much of Scratch's documentation as well.	Free
Tynker Inspired by Scratch, Tynker has a dashboard to allow teachers to create a more structured way of teaching code with visual blocks. Includes assessment, classroom management, lesson plans, and a built-in tutor.	Free to $399 for class account (30 students)

Learn Specific Coding Languages

Product	Price
Code Avengers In-browser exercises and courses in JavaScript, HTML5, CSS3 and Python. Introductory courses are free, with intermediate and advanced courses for $29-$39.	Free to $39 for advanced lessons
Codecademy Offers free coding courses and curriculum resources including lesson plans to help teachers plan computer science classes. Exercises are done in browser and checked automatically for accuracy.	Free
CodeHS Karel the Dog just got some new tricks! CodeHS offers full year courses to teach Introduction to Computer Science in JavaScript, AP Computer Science in Java, and a professional development course for teachers.	Free; contact CodeHS for school subscription
HTML5 Rocks Online resource with tutorials, demos, and sample work in HTML5. Supplementary resource for educators teaching the language.	Free
Khan Academy Users watch videos, do exercises and play with sample code to learn JavaScript programming basics. Completely browser-based with an interactive player/editor.	Free
KidsRuby This free, downloadable program teaches kids Ruby and can be used completely offline. KidsRuby includes resources from other programs like Hackety Hack and Ruby Warrior. It can be installed on Mac, Linux, Windows, and even Raspberry Pi.	Free
MIT OpenCourseWare This initiative by MIT puts all of the course materials from the university's undergraduate and graduate courses online. This includes syllabi, reading lists, and sometimes practice questions and video lectures. Covers many formal programming languages and offers advanced theory classes as well. Recommended for students who are self-motivated.	Free
Mozilla Thimble Sample websites with annotations guiding students to change variables to impact aesthetics and usability. Instructors will want to create their own lessons around the content.	Free

Games—and Tools to Code Your Own Games

Product	Price
Code Combat In-browser, multiplayer live coding game set in a fantasy world. You play as a wizard who navigates obstacles and battles enemies using Javascript.	Free for first course; additional courses require one-time fee
Globaloria Blended-learning courses that teach students to design and code educational games using Flash Actionscript, Unity3D, JavaScript, and more. Used as standalone courses or to supplement core **classes.**	Free. Contact Globaloria about school subscription.
Hakitzu This iPad game teaches the fundamentals of JavaScript by allowing players to program robots to compete in arena battles.	Free (in-app purchases available)
JS Dares A collection of JavaScript lessons that go from teaching a student about basic syntax to helping them recreate working games. Browser-based and completely free.	Free
Kodable Kodable is a freemium educational iPad game offering a kid-friendly introduction to programming concepts and problem solving. For kids ages 5 and up.	Free to $6.99; school pricing available
Kodu Created by Microsoft, this program uses a visual language to create games. While the PC version is free, Xbox 360 users can pick up a copy for $5.	Free
Stencyl Game creation software that allows users to make playable apps for iOS, Android, HTML5, Window, and Mac. The game logic is programmed with visual blocks. The official site has forums and a crash course to get you started.	Free

Learn to Program Hardware

Product	Price
Arduino A popular choice for hands-on learners who want their code to interact with the real world. Can be used for creating a range of projects in the Arduino Code programming language--from light up coffee tables to robots. Extensive documentation of projects online at websites like Instructables. Instructors take note that LEDs, motors, and sensors cost extra. Fairly involved hardware and programming environment setup time.	$25+
Lego Mindstorms EV3 The ubiquitous blocks from Denmark get a technological upgrade. This set allows users to create and program robots through a visual programming language. Big for hands-on learning (with a big price tag to match). Instructors keep in mind that projects require construction and programming time. Support can be found on the Mindstorms forum. Windows and Mac compatible.	$350
Piper Piper combines Minecraft, Raspberry Pis and circuit boards—all in a box. The kit comes with a Raspberry Pi board, a 7-inch LCD display, a power bank, and a hodgepodge of breadboards, wires and buttons. Designed for kids of all ages, Piper challenges players to solve virtual puzzles in Minecraft by using the physical circuit controller to build bridges and switches.	$250
Primo Primo literally takes the concept of "block coding" to create an Arduino-powered toy set that includes a plywood board, a wooden robot, and color-coded blocks that each instruct one move that Cubetto can make.	£170 (currently on backorder)
Raspberry Pi This credit card-sized single board computer packs a punch! The Pi can be used for hands-on fun like an Arduino and is powerful enough to run a version of Minecraft. eLinux.org has a wealth of tutorials and projects for the tiny titan of the "Maker" world. Instructors take note that LEDs, motors, and sensors cost extra.	$5+
Sphero Let's get rolling! Sphero and sidekick Ollie are interactive spherical robots that you can program on your iOS, Android and Windows devices. There are dozens of apps available, as well as a growing educator community. These may be the droids you are looking for.	$100+

Wanna Get Serious? Try a Course!

Product	Price
Code School Offers full courses in JavaScript, HTML, CSS, Ruby, and iOS. Students will learn through video and practice coding in their browser--no downloads required! (Acquired by Pluralsight but still in operation.)	$29/mo
Coursera Beginning courses in JavaScript, Python, SQL and general computer science. Also offers higher-level logic courses in topics like Data Science, Artificial Intelligence, and Computational Neuroscience. Note that classes have start and end dates. Founded by Stanford computer science professors, Andrew Ng and Daphne Koller.	Free
edX Covers languages like Python, Ruby, C++ as well as higher level classes in Artificial Intelligence and Computer Graphics. Classes are taught through video, PDFs, and tutorials. Students answer problem sets and take tests online. Discussion boards connect students with professors and each other. Note that courses have specific start and end dates.	Free
Envato Tuts+ Full courses in JavaScript, HTML, CSS, Ruby, and other web development tools. Subscriptions are $15/month with discounts for groups.	$15/mo
Lynda.com A collection of video tutorials covering a wide variety of formal coding languages. Beginners and advanced users alike can find lessons to suit their needs. Access to videos costs $25/month; users can access videos and exercise files for $37.50/month. Enterprise licenses are available for schools/districts.	$25+/mo

Chapter 3

CODING CURRICULUM DEVELOPMENT

"Children must be taught how to think,
not what to think."

~Margaret Mead

The courses I develop are more highly effective with two layers of tasks for the students working simultaneously at their pace on both. Due dates are still present and enforced; but the students have the ability to work on tasks in either "layer."

Layer 1
I use CodeHS to deliver lessons and curriculum. They work on these to get the information and concepts down. These are the learning opportunities that are not required for grades, but they really are required because I won't answer questions that are covered in the lessons unless students prove they have reviewed the lessons in CodeHS, first.

Layer 2
Projects! I use projects as the "meat" of the course. When students engage in Project-Based Learning activities, their engagement skyrockets and their knowledge acquisition and long-term learning is much greater. This is where they struggle, work the problem, find out the outside connections, learn who they are as a learner, etc.

Both layers are covered in this chapter separately, but the controlled chaos is where the magic happens! Students have the freedom to work on what they need at the time. The difference is that the teacher is there to guide them along the right path.

Coding & The Standards

Coding meets many of the academic standards outlined by local districts, counties, states and national governing bodies. While this handbook would be too long if I provided a correlation guide for each governing body, I have provided an example below as to how these lessons would relate to the Common Core State Standards (Adapted from Linney, 2015). This text is to be used as a sample only, realizing that not all states are participants in the Common Core State Standards Initiative.

I might suggest using the ISTE Standards for states that might not have direct correlations to a coding curriculum. The ISTE standards can be found at: https://www.iste.org/standards/for-students

Mathematics Standards Correlation

MP.1: *K-8	Make sense of problems and persevere in solving them.	In programming activities, students must persevere in problem solving.
NBT.1: *2-5	Place value and decimal use (generally; but scaled by grade level)	Use wait blocks and movement blocks in programs like Scratch and Tynker to differentiate between .01, .1, 1, and 10 seconds.
4.OA.5	Generate and analyze patterns	Have students create drawings in programs that repeat a pattern. This can be done with the "repeat" (a.k.a. "loop") block. Students can demonstrate their understanding of multiplicative procedures and patterns that follow a specific rule.
4.MD.5 and 4.MD.6	Geometric measurement: understand concepts of volume.	Use studio.code.org or their *Frozen*-themed puzzles to teach students about angle measurements.
5.G.1, 5.G.2, and 6.G.3	Graph points on the coordinate plane to solve real-world and mathematical problems. Solve real-world mathematical problems involving area, surface area, and volume.	In Scratch, choose "Backdrop" and, under "Categories," click "Other." The last backdrop in "Other" is an XY grid. Students can use this grid to graph points and draw shapes within the coordinate system.
6.NS.5, 6.NS.6, and 6.NS.7	Apply and extend previous understandings of numbers to the system of rational numbers.	Have students build programs where actors (or sprites) move to specific points on a coordinate plane, based on an action (a conditional).

English Language Arts/Literacy Standards Correlation

RI.3: *K-5	Explain the relationships or interactions between two or more individuals, events, ideas, or concepts in a historical, scientific, or technical text based on specific information in the text.	Have students describe what would happen if the blocks in a program went in a specific order. Identify cause-and-effect relationships by using "if this, then. . ." blocks.
RI.5: *2-4	Compare and contrast the overall structure (e.g., chronology, comparison, cause/effect, problem/solution) of events, ideas, concepts, or information in two or more texts.	Locate answers to a question using keywords, sidebars, and glossaries. (Programming tools use menus and categories to organize blocks.)
SL.5: *2-5	Engage effectively in a range of collaborative discussions with diverse partners building on other's ideas and expressing their own clearly.	Create digital stories in programming platforms such as Scratch and Tynker, changing the scene (background) between events. Create tutorials on how to advance through a programming level.
W.2 and WHST.2: *K-8	Write informative/explanatory texts to examine and convey complex ideas and information clearly and accurately through the effective selection, organization, and analysis of content. Write informative/explanatory texts, including the narration of historical events, scientific procedures/experiments, or technical processes.	Compose a tutorial on how to advance through a level/stage, or how to animate a character. Write a comparative analysis, analyzing two different coding platforms or languages.
RST.3 and RST.4: *6-8	Follow precisely a multistep procedure when carrying out experiments, taking measurements, or performing technical tasks. Determine the meaning of symbols, key terms, and other domain-specific words and phrases as they are used in a specific scientific or technical context relevant to *grades 6-8 texts and topics.*	Complete JavaScript tutorials in Khan Academy.

Preparing Lessons

Project-Based Learning

Much has been written on the subject of project and problem based learning. Teaching coding past the beginner stages fits into this perspective very well. Let go and let the students flourish.

True Project Based Learning (PBL) challenges students to acquire deeper knowledge of a concept by establishing connections outside their classroom. According to the research on PBL, the main tenets are to create real world connections, develop critical thinking skills, foster structured collaboration, motivate student driven work, and enable a multifaceted approach.

Similarly, coding applies all of these core tenets, as programs require logical thinking, teamwork, a variety of tools, and –most importantly – perseverance on the part of the student. Consider the potential of applying the challenges of coding to the proven successful tenets of PBL.

PBL Tenet #1: Create Real World Connections

Coding Application: Find a solution to a problem by creating an App or Website.

Using PBL in my classroom, students are encouraged to connect with their community. They are challenged them to create an iPhone App that fulfilled a need in order to model what happens in real world programming.

Students have created student orientation apps, transportation apps and parking apps. The struggles were real; but perseverance and problem-solving were at the root of these real-world problems.

PBL Tenet #2: Foster Critical Thinking

Much like PBL migrates learning away from worksheets and reports, coding is becoming less about the syntax, or programming language, and more about the logic needed to layout the solution. Some programs, such as Scratch, do not even use a language but rather have students drag-and-drop widgets into a specific order to make a program. The more important aspect of a coding project is that the students gain the bigger picture of how their program can potentially solve the problem at hand rather than master the specific coding languages.

PBL Tenet #3: Structured Collaboration
Coding application: Coding creates learning communities

Collaboration comes natural in coding as questions arise about the technical aspects of the projects. Students seek answers and advice from their peers inside the classroom as well as from outside sources, such as programming forums, ultimately creating a learning community.

Students work not only with the departments, individuals, etc. for the project they have decided to attempt. They also work with stakeholders (customers, demographics, data) and with their peers in the classroom to assist in building community projects where their class members are their consultants.

PBL Tenet #4: Student Driven
Coding application: Perseverance and self-teaching are important skills learned through coding. Students are on their own for most of the time to experience real struggle and develop tremendous grit.

Completing a program means that all of the functions effectively work. Finding all of the hiccups, and then resolving them, can be a painful and frustrating process. However, the satisfaction of creating a functioning program is fulfilling and builds confidence. Furthermore, in a successful community project, students can be empowered by seeing their apps make a difference.

PBL Tenet #5: Multifaceted approach
Coding application: A programming language is only one part of an app or website
Many students walk away from their projects, only to return when they have thought about it for a while.

By the end of a coding project, a student has identified a problem, researched, determined a solution, and laid out a plan – all before the "coding" begins. Students need to understand how people might use their program more than how to code it. This requires interacting with peers, experts, and community members to test and retest.

Through Project Based Learning and coding, students have the potential to gain a deeper level of understanding of not only programming, but also the topics involved in the content of their application. The vested time and interest into such an undertaking, and the fulfillment of creating a meaningful product with an impact on their community, provides students with an authentic learning opportunity.
Adapted from (Wilson, n.d.)

PBL Design Elements

The Buck Institute (2015), highlights several important features of Effective PBL. I have provided a summary to each below. The full rubric can be viewed on their website at: https://goo.gl/8oyvhz

Key Knowledge, Understanding & Success

Start by asking yourself, what are the three or four things students must absolutely learn during the course of the project. This will probably break down later into smaller skills along the way. It is best to outline these at the outset before getting overwhelmed by all the possibilities.

Challenging Problem or Question

While most educators prefer a question or problem to solve, I like have a project title. I don't try to confine my projects by seeking a question; but more by learning the process and achieving outcomes. I find that when I phrase things as questions, my students are confused or overwhelmed by trying to figure it out right away. Such is the testing generation that we are raising. Answer quick and move on. I like when they take it slow to not necessarily seek an answer but to develop a passion.

Sustained Inquiry

A fantastic project has the element of driving more questions from the students, not from me. The project has to be authentic, involve real-world tasks, tools and quality standards. It has to have the ability to make a real impact on the world or speak to the passions of the students. The current generation of students does not seek to volunteer at a soup kitchen; they seek to end the need for soup kitchens entirely. They can do that with coding! Make it as real as possible. If you don't know, call in an expert on Google Hangouts.

Student Voice & Choice

Previously, while establishing rules, I discussed the idea that we, "Never fear creativity!" Giving students the opportunity explore other avenues of providing an outcome is so very important to fostering the self-driven student. I have to frame this for myself as looking for all the reasons I should say, "Yes" and not "No." It forces me to consider their proposal. I must maintain that they are learning; but they will decide the path. Maria Montessori would be so proud!

Reflection

As I move through the classroom speaking to students in groups or working individually, among all the other things I am doing (correcting issues, behavior modification, attendance, etc.) I engage my students in dialogue to focus students on their metacognitive skills. I ask the following questions of my students on a regular basis:

- How did you learn that?
- Walk me through the steps you used to problem-solve that issue.
- Did you find it difficult to start on this? What was the most challenging part of the last 3 days in class?
- How far along are you? Do you need my assistance with anything?
- If you were going to hire me to help with the project, what would you have me do?

Their answers sometimes surprise me. Usually, the students are suspicious of this in the beginning of the year. Most of them only get asked those questions when they are about to get in trouble. As the year goes on, they seem to enjoy and anticipate the questions. They learn to brag a little about themselves and their confidence soars. In so many classrooms, we have removed this in the surge forward to "cover" the curriculum.

Critique & Revision

Students are encouraged to talk to each other and collaborate. They should be showing off their projects to the groups or individuals in class on a regular basis. Additionally, the platform I use for the main lessons includes all the instructional materials in a flipped manner. Therefore, I am available to move around the room and provide feedback on a daily basis. However, the big critique and revision process takes place a week or so before the due date. That process is included in the section *Student Critique Exercises* on *page 64*.

Public Product

Students are encouraged to share their work with others outside the classroom on a regular basis. Administration is invited for presentations to assist in the feedback process. Here are some ideas for getting your students work out into the community:

- Host a Tech Night each quarter, semester or year where students can exhibit their work.
- Have a panel of experts join the class via Google Hangouts and provide feedback or sponsorship to taking the idea into the bigger scale. (Think: Shark Tank)
- Encourage students to release their projects, apps or other ideas publicly in the forums for credit or extra-credit. This is easy to do with platforms such as Scratch or Snap.
- Inject Student-led, Parent Conferences into your practice.
- Enter projects in contests and events that support student coding.

The public product is such an important step. It signals to students that this is about more than just the grade. This almost raises the stakes for the student much larger than the grade. I found that only my grade motivated students cared about the grade. Most students wanted to participate in the events we were running so they worked harder than if it were just for a grade.

PBL Teaching Practices

The Buck Institute (2015), highlights several important features of Effective PBL teaching practices. I have provided a summary to each below. The full rubric can be viewed on their website at: https://goo.gl/6NgfwX

Design & Plan

This should be a detailed plan throughout the project that includes scaffolding and assessing throughout. This plan should also take into account all the elements of the project as described in the previous section. Resources also should be included in the plan and be allocated and developed prior to implementation.

Align to Standards

Since 1996, there has been increasing attention in developing lessons that focus on standards and accountability. I find a great deal of assistance in using the ISTE (International Society for Technology in Education) standards (https://goo.gl/TxfD6k). However, many of the PBL lessons you will teach in a technology classroom can meet standards outside of the technology arena. There is a guide to the most frequently used national standards in the section Coding & The Standards on page 46. Of course, standards can be more localized by state, territory or local council. Be sure to check those, too.

Build to Culture

This is the part of the process where you establish procedure for what you want your students doing, what you want them learning and how you make them yearn for the content. The quote that drives me is:

> *"If you want to build a ship, don't drum up the men to gather wood, divide the work and give orders. Instead, teach them to yearn for the vast and endless sea."*
>
> ~Antoine de Saint-Exupery

The students should be working together in collaboration between the educator and each other in a series of established norms to create a positive, learner-directed work environment. This severely cuts back on behavior issues, motivation issues. Much of this book is littered with small examples on how to create that environment.

Manage Activities

Formative assessment, both formal and informal, are arranged ahead of time and a schedule is produced for students to manage their own time. Routines are present and self-directed for students to maximize productivity. In my classroom, there was a looped presentation on the screen that had the day's agenda, announcements, featured students/projects, upcoming assignments or motivational quotes. No more than 5 slides that go 20 seconds each. Students would come in and read the slides and get to work. The key is training them for the, "I don't know what I am supposed to be doing" statement. Never answer that question, simply point them to the resources.

Scaffold Student Learning

We must not forget what Vygotsky taught us. We want to keep our learners in the *zone of proximal development*. They should be challenged, but not frustrated. I always try to remember that they should feel uneasy; but not feeling like they want to quit. This is why I use an online flipped model (or in-flip) in my classroom. This frees me up to remediate when necessary. Students work at their own pace; but I am present to slow them down, coach them or remediate a lesson if they are stuck.

Assess Student Learning

You will find multiple points of assessment throughout. Students do work in the online module through CodeHS. They receive completion grades and quiz scores are drawn out to measure individual progress. Students also produce both individual projects and group projects at different times throughout the school year. Each of those projects usually has a component for formative assessment throughout. Additionally, I am speaking with most of them each day. I have more points of contact for individualized, informal assessment.

Engage & Coach

It is true that I could sit at my desk and grade papers, read the paper, finally see the end to my inbox, etc. However, it is the engagement that teaches me so much about my students. The students' questions reveal points for instructional improvement, ways to support them as they grow, convey high expectations, etc.

I so cherish this time with students. I used to teach the way I was taught. That worked for me why wouldn't it work for them. Then I realized I could be in two places at the same time. That changed everything! I have been able to make a far great impact on my students learning by shifting things and becoming a coach, mentor and facilitator. I become a member of the class and there is really nobody in charge. The role is rarely needed, because we are a community.

> The following planning template has the elements discussed in the last two sections. This is also available to you on the Schoology page in electronic form.

PBL Instructional Planning Template

Backward Design Instructional Planning Template	
Preliminary Planning Format	
Unit Title:	**Grade Level(s)**
Subject(s)/Topic Area(s)	

Stage 1 – Identify Desired Results	
Driving Questions, Outcomes or Problems: (Include Standards Correlations, if applicable)	
Direct Goals, Standards, and Objectives:	**Indirect Goals, Standards, and Objectives:**
Standards Correlations	**Final Product Summary (Summative Assessment)**

Stage 2 – Assessment Evidence

Formative Assessments (List All):

Stage 3 – Project Timeline & Resources

At the end of this planning, I prefer to create a handout (1-4 pages) with a summary for the students, the timeline, the rubrics and the requirements of the Summative Assessment. This allows them to see up front where we are going and how we are going to get there. Don't allow yourself to get stuck in any one place in the beginning. As ideas come to you write them down...this is a graphic organizer; not a requirement.

App Development Project Example

Project Summary

For this project, you will be creating an
app of your choice to solve a situation
of convenience, information delivery,
etc. You will work on the project in small
weekly assignments leading up to the final
project. This will allow you to have
feedback along the way and also to keep
you on track with the size of this project.

The project requires you to write a
significant amount of information for me
to show evidence of learning and working
the process. You should include the
weekly assignments in the final write-
up. This is the intention of the weekly assignments. Be sure to fix them up based on the
feedback you receive from the original turn-in.

You do NOT have to build a working app. You simply have to graphically represent the
final product with explanations of how the functions and interactions would
respond. You should also define the functionality of each of the screens of the app.

Deliverables

All teams must create the following items and have them posted on their Google Site.

- A Complete Google Site with all the required information.
- An analysis of competitors/similar products apps.
- A Word document with all the team members' names on them and a link
  to your Google Site (this must be turned in on Schoology).
- Paragraphs of information analyzing the current site and why it is or is
  not sound in the design principals outlined in the McKay text.
- Wireframe drawings of the new app with explanation detailing why you
  decided to add/remove/improve current navigation, controls, design, etc.
- The Google Site should be a solid case for change by the company.
- Be sure to evaluate your own project based on the rubric posted on
  Schoology.

For your final project, you will design a user experience and make suggestions for improvement to the interactive elements. You will use the McKay text to make justification for the changes you are proposing. You will post your details on a Google Site. Please see the project handout in the Final Exam folder for details.

The project should be a minimum of four major sections:

1. What the interface looked like before (include screenshots) and why this does not match the standards of UI design.

2. Include the personas for different user types that would be using the site and discuss how these people will be addressed in the re-design process.

3. Analysis of what should be changed and justification as to why it should change based on your reading and class work.

4. A new design with the justification of why you chose those new designs.

Each of these sections can be broken down by sections of the interface. Keep it simple. This project can grow very large, very fast!

Submit the link Google Site in a word document with all your group members' names on them.

Criteria	Grading Scale			
Criteria	**Grading Scale**			
Portfolio Site Setup The site is setup to address many of the UI principles for ease of use and understanding.	**3** Excellent	**2** Good	**1** Satisfactory	
Analysis of Competitive/Similar Products The team adequately analyzed the original UI for design, user-centered and effective communication.	**4** Excellent	**3** Good	**2** Satisfactory	**1** Needs Improvement
New Design UI The UI is designed well and screenshots are present and clean.	**6** Excellent	**4** Good	**2** Satisfactory	**1** Needs Improvement
Justification for New UI Choices Paragraphs are present and organized in a way that provide clarity to the decisions the group made in the proposed changes.	**6** Excellent	**4** Good	**2** Satisfactory	**1** Needs Improvement
Core Principles of UI New design adheres to the Core Principles of UI on pgs. 15-16 of the McKay text.	**4** Excellent	**3** Good	**2** Satisfactory	**1** Needs Improvement
Group Interaction and Participation Each group was able to solve agreement issues, add value to the product and engage all group members.	**4** Excellent	**3** Good	**2** Satisfactory	**1** Needs Improvement
User Profile Consideration Strong evidence is shown to support the consideration of all users that would be interacting and communicating through this UI.	**4** Excellent	**3** Good	**2** Satisfactory	**1** Needs Improvement
Explanation of Interactions in UI Properly defined and explained how each of the functions would work and how end users could expect things to behave when using features and interactions in the app.	**6** Excellent	**4** Good	**2** Satisfactory	**1** Needs Improvement
Usefulness The app proposed and selected for design proves to be useful to the intended audience.	**4** Excellent	**3** Good	**2** Satisfactory	**1** Needs Improvement

Total pts: 41

CodeHS
codehs.com/

CodeHS's goal "is to spread the knowledge of computer science by offering well-crafted instructional materials supported by continuously by the quality, personal attention of [their] enthusiastic tutors. [They] believe that everyone has the ability to learn computer science, and [they] want to help them do so (CodeHS, n.d.)."

CodeHS is a great tool for teaching computer science as a dedicated course. While the curriculum is written for high school students, their scope and sequence could be adapted to a middle school course, as well. The service is free for a few year-long courses. The lesson plans, scope and sequence, and sample syllabi are all included in the free version. There is a paid version that has a built-in gradebook, handouts and problem guides. In short, you are purchasing the curricula for many courses in a built in LMS. At the time of this printing, their website was stating a $2,500 starting package for school subscriptions.

Scope & Sequence
Here is an excerpt of their sample CodeHS syllabus for 60-Minute High School Class, Intro to CS. Find the full syllabus: https://codehs.com/syllabus/sample

At a Glance

General Topic	Days
Programming with Karel	1 - 34
Basic Javascript and Graphics	34 - 88
Animation and Games	89 - 123
Project: Breakout	123 - 125
Basic Data Structures	125 - 160

Sample Sequence of Lessons

Day	Activities	Terms	Discussion Questions
39	Basic User Input Grocery Store Basic Math in JavaScript Basic Math in JavaScript	Integer	What is user input? How can user input be used in a program?
40	Basic Math in JavaScript Quiz Simple Calculator Dollars to Pounds Dividing Up Groups		
41	T-Shirt Shop Running Speed Using Graphics in JavaScript	Variable Integer Constant	How can variables be used to perform computation? Can you give an example of a simple math problem using variables instead of hard-coded values?
42	Graphics JavaScript Graphics Quiz Graphics Hello World Blue Circle Red Rectangle 8 Ball		
43	French Flag Snowman Booleans Booleans	Canvas	Why would it be useful to store values in a variable? What advantages does this have over hard-coding values in a program?

How can variables be used with `getWidth()` and `getHeight()` to find the dimensions of the canvas? |

Individual Lesson Plan from CodeHS

Lesson Breakdown

Instructional Day	18	Lesson Title	How can we use Javascript make our program print out a message?

Description	Javascript uses the function println to print a message to the screen.
Prior Knowledge	All Karel challenges completed
Planning Notes	At this point in the curriculum, students should have completed all Karel World challenges in order to move on to Basic Javascript and Animation. If you find that students are having difficulty achieving this, allow time for them to finish challenges and engage in the videos and example exercises of the next module. It is important that students have a proficient understanding of functions as well as problem decomposition before beginning Basic Javascript. The initial JavaScript problems are much easier than the last Karel Challenges. Lastly, since the lesson objectives are relatively few, this lesson may be combined with the *Variables* lesson.
Teaching Learning Strategies	<ul><li>Do Now: *Define the word <u>interactive</u>. What makes a computer program or application interactive? Think of five applications or programs that allow you to interact with it. What makes them interactive?*</li><li>Discuss the Do Now with students by generating a list of definitions of the word <u>interactive,</u> characteristics of interactive programs, and names of these programs.</li><li>Push students to think about the similarities of interactive programs and how these features might be programmed based on what they know from learning about Karel.</li><li>Watch *Hello World* video.</li><li>Pause video intermittently top point out the println function and the ("My name is Jeremy").</li><li>Direct student to explore more about JavaScript by examining the *Hello World* example.</li><li>Encourage students to examine the new syntax introduced by removing the quotation marks around the Hello world. Discuss the functionality and importance of quotation marks in attempting to print a message on the screen.</li><li>Prompt students to inquire what might happen if they wanted to print a third message.</li><li>Students work individually or in pairs to complete *Your Name*</li></ul>

	and Hobby.
Assessment and Evaluations	Exercise 2.4
Solution Guides	- <u>Your Name and Hobby</u>

Handouts & Resources (Example Exercises/Videos)	*Hello World* video *Hello World*	**CodeHS Exercises**	*Your Name and Hobby*

Vocabulary	println()
Homework	

Modifications

Advanced Students	**Special Edu Students**	**Struggling Readers/English Language Learners**
• Students may create a program in the Sandbox.	• Modify Do Now that asks student how a popular website like Facebook or Gmail allow the user to type or click on the screen. Have student describe the process. • Allow students to write what they would like their message to read on paper first. • Ask student where they might place their message in the code.	• Provide a definition for the word *interactive* and allow student to generate synonyms for the word. • Provide a fill-in-the-blank for the Do Now that requires the student to use the word *interactive* in describing why a particular program is interactive.

Student Critique Exercises

When teaching coding exercises, or any other tech lesson, one of my largest successes comes from empowering the students to provide feedback. The model used in class comes from an adaptation of the AFI Screen Education Handbook (American Film Institute, 2006). The process takes a class period or two (depending on the size and detail of the project); but is time well spent in the process.

How it Works

Here are the best practices for implementation.

Step 1 – PREPARATION: Lie to the Students!

Well, it's only a small white lie in their best interests. Give them a due date prior to the "real" due date. This will make sense in a after you read on in the final step!

Step 2 – CRITIQUE: Providing Constructive Feedback

A. Define the roles of students as follows:
- Presenter – the spokesperson for the group showing its project for the purpose of receiving information. They should present the good, the bad and the ugly.
- Facilitator – the student who volunteers to work the steps of the process. They will remain the facilitator through the entire process.
- Time-Keeper – A student appointed to keep the presentations on time.

B. Phase 1 – Overview: The first 5 minutes the group's presenter gives a quick overview of the work and shows the group's project.

C. Phase 2 – Clarifying Questions: The facilitator explains that there will be 3 minutes for the audience to ask clarifying questions of the group. Clarifying questions are for the benefit of the member asking the question. These are questions are who, what, where, when, and how; but not why.

D. Phase 3 – Probing Questions – The facilitator now gives 7 minutes for the why questions. Probing questions are for the benefit of the group presenting to further refine their project.

E. Phase 4 – Audience Discussion: The facilitator asks the presenting group or individual to listen only. The audience will talk about the presentation in the third person, as if the group was not present, so that a rich analysis can be offered. Start with the positives. Fill in the gaps and goals that may have been missed.

F. Phase 5 – Facilitator Summary: The facilitator summarizes the findings of the successes and offers the next steps to revise based on the feedback provided by the audience. This process is allotted 2 minutes.

G. Phase 6 – Presenter Response: The presenter and/or their group responds to the feedback. This is their reflection on the significant ideas and new thoughts received from listening to the classroom community feedback. Three minutes are allotted for this process.

H. Phase 7 – Teacher Review: Only when all groups have gone through the process, the teacher leads a debriefing about the groups' observations of the process. It is important that during the process above the teacher is fairly silent. It is only appropriate to provide feedback if the class seeks your clarification of understanding or if the students need coaching on providing constructive feedback. This is the students process, so let them have it. This review should only be 5 minutes long.

Phase	Time Allotted
Phase 1: Overview	5 minutes
Phase 2: Clarifying Questions	3 minutes
Phase 3: Probing Questions	7 minutes
Phase 4: Audience Discussion	5 minutes
Phase 5: Facilitator Summary	2 minutes
Phase 6: Presenter Response	3 minutes
Phase 7: Teacher Review	5 minutes
Total	30 minutes*

* The process will take longer the first time. The times do not have to remain at the suggested times. Make accommodations for the project, student performance, etc.

Step 3 – REWORK: Grace!

This is where the lie pays off. Once every group goes through the process, give them a few days to rework the projects based on the group feedback process. You will evaluate the project for assessment on the final due date.

Students Not Working? Good! They still stand up and present nothing...but the facilitator is the one applying the pressure (not you). The time keeper still holds the group to the time allotted for each step (again, not you). So, the class sits in silence waiting for something. They will bail themselves out a few times talking about "what might have been;" and that is fine. They will feel the pressure of not getting their work done and being held accountable for their decisions/distractions.

Students are allowed to be tough on those presenting; just not rude! Questions such as:

"Why aren't you prepared?"

"Why didn't you do the project?"

"Why are you wasting our time?"

These questions are allowed to be asked and the student(s) presenting are required to answer them.

Why it Works

↓ Students are stricter and much tougher on each other than you can ever be.

↓ Even if students are not all doing the same exact assignment and taking the same learning path, they all learn the content! You will be amazed at the depth of knowledge acquisition and retention that your students will display.

↓ Most learning disabilities almost disappear, since most students are learning by doing things that match their ability.

↓ Students stay focused on tasks for unbelievable amounts of time and even begin to use their breaks, recess, and lunchtime to work on material they know will be accessed by a real audience.

↓ You will be amazed at what your students can do when you stop running things from the front of the room. You will find that you have more time for one-on-one work, since you act as a docent, observer and facilitator.

↓ The only "drawback" to the students is that they can no longer fade into the background or fake their way to an A+.

Chapter 4

PULLING IT ALL TOGETHER

"Whether you want to uncover the secrets of the universe,
or you want to pursue a career in the 21st century,
basic computer programming is an essential skill to learn."

~Stephen Hawking

The following chapter is a collection of technical resources for you to choose from in pulling all the pieces of the book together. It is really a cafeteria of ideas of ways to add to your collection of lessons or bring your content online. Much of the following is borrowed from my work on flipped classrooms. The flipped classroom has become so much a part of my practice and I would never consider going back.

Additionally, this chapter provides examples of lessons and how my year might be structured. Included are sample project lessons and timelines for you to manipulate any way that fits you and your students. You are free to take what you like and leave the rest.

Women in Coding

Reshma Saujani poses a profound hypothesis from her own experiences in life in comparison to working with young adolescents to teach them to code. In her TED speech (2016) she presents the idea that women are conditioned to be perfect in juxtaposition to men being taught to be brave. She provides several examples throughout the Ted talk, but one sticks out as it relates to coding in the classroom and why we see more males drawn toward the field of study.

Ms. Saujani tells the story of one female student who signaled the teacher after what appeared to be a significant amount of time staring at the screen. She explained that she did not understand what she was supposed to do or where to get started. The teacher, at first glance, is faced with the issue of a student who appears to have done nothing. However, she hits the undo button a few times and notices that she has attempted several times; but deleted it each time. For the female student, it was perfection or bust.

In my own reflection, I wonder how many times I made the quick judgement that the student was not motivated, wasn't paying attention, was looking for attention or just wanted to get under my skin. The undo button is such a quick way to get an idea of attempts. Later, after visiting several schools as a politician, she opened her organization, Girls Who Code

(girlswhocode.com). This is a wonderful resource for young women to connect with each other.

Figure 2 - girlswhocode.com

The interesting part of the hypothesis is that it does not go where research has gone before to compare the abilities, cognitive fortitude or physical characteristic differences between men and women; but to look at the social conditioning that occurs that may be a reason for the gap. Much work must be done in the field to support growing a diverse workforce in the field of coding. It must be mentioned that women are not the only left

out of the coding experience. Individuals of color are also left out. Basically, the majority group in coding positions are white males. That must change.

The larger question becomes, "What else can we do to support young women and persons of color as they explore the field of programming and coding?" There must be a culture change within the field itself. However, without interested, qualified candidates; this does not happen. Therefore, it is up to us as educators to make sure students have options to continue the study into high school and/or college.

Here is a small list of suggestions to explore which might help you address diversity in the coding field.

- Never let students blame themselves for broken code. This insures that young women break the conditioning that they are what is wrong. (See Establishing Classroom Rules section on page 8)

- Bring in experts, or professionals, in the field to speak to your students who are women or persons of color. Make sure that the students see the faces of people in the field that represent the diversity we seek.

- Allow students to choose project ideas or modifications that speak to a positive social change locally, nationally or globally.

- Use Google Hangouts, or similar video conferencing tools, to stretch to markets that will represent diversity and work with those individuals for project ideas, guest speakers, guest critiques, etc.

- Be honest with students that this is a field dominated by white males; but the field is seeking talented women and people of color.

Video Link: Reshma Saujani – Teach Bravery; Not Perfection
Found in the Schoology Page – Module 4 Folder (edited video)

Full video can be found at:
https://www.ted.com/talks/reshma_saujani_teach_girls_bravery_not_perfection

Scope & Sequence

As I travel around the country and abroad, speaking on various technology integration topics, the resounding feedback I receive is related to the practical, common sense approach I take to such a complex and overwhelming task. In the following graphic, I will try to highlight the overview of how I layout a curriculum. In the following section, Project Samples, you will find samples of larger projects. Also, keep in mind that this is a framework and is open to change and evolution. Please substitute and change things to fit the needs of your instructional goals.

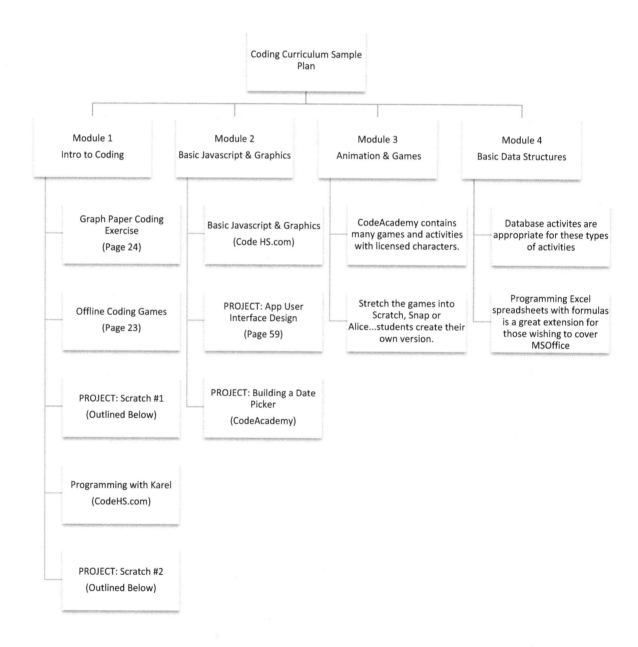

Project Samples

Projects are built like gymnastics or figure skating routines. Give the students the requirements and let them build the routine.

Project #1: Scratch Intro

Students will focus on the Movement and Control commands in Scratch. Very little direct instruction will occur and students will be directed to the tutorials in Scratch. Students should create an account on Scratch so that they can save their work from period to period. Students under the age of 13 will need to provide a parent email address for COPA compliance.

Requirements
- Sprite must move at least three times
- Sprint must interact w/ the environment and cause something to occur as a result of the interaction.
- The project should convey a small story scene.

Objectives
- Discover the logic of coding (without the syntax) in the Scratch platform.
- Build a series of instructions to control the sprite and its interactions on the screen (your first program).
- Create a small scene using only instructions provided in the Scratch platform.

Project #2:

Students will focus on the Movement and Control commands in Scratch, again. However, the requirements this time have been enhanced a bit. The objectives remain the same since students are relatively new to coding and have been working in CodeHS. The difference in platform is a bit of a shift for them, so the project objectives stay the same, but the requirements change.

Requirements
- You must use 2 or more sprites
- Each sprite must move at least three times
- Sprint must interact w/ each other and cause something to occur as a result of the interaction
- The project should convey a small story scene (longer than the previous project).

Objectives
- Discover the logic of coding (without the syntax) in the Scratch platform.
- Build a series of instructions to control the sprite and its interactions on the screen (your first program).
- Create a small scene using only instructions provided in the Scratch platform.

Fail Fast & Solutions-Based Thinking

As you can imagine, students are always maxing out their "Zone of Proximal Development," as Vygotsky would say. They are living the zone of frustration. Here is where they learn grit, determination and perseverance (and yes, empathy, too!).

Nothing is worse than the group that throws out the baby with the bathwater at the end of the project timeline. They have hit the wall and cannot move any further. There are sometimes where I can't assist them out of the issue, either. Usually, it is the planning at prototyping that they saved for the end, and it is just not happening.

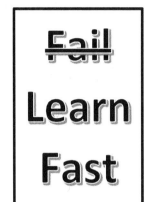

To prevent this from happening, I encourage my students to "Fail Fast" from the outset of the project. Fail fast is a concept that applies to the little issues that pop up along the project journey. The fail fast is about trying something out and then accepting, rejecting or continue testing the results. If you accept the results and they are not how you anticipated things going, you pivot! This is the magic sauce when it comes to students.

When an issue occurs, high-performing students usually panic. They are in competition to show you how smart they are and when tested, they curl up in mental paralysis. This almost looks like a 4-year-old tantrum (no offense to toddlers). When low-performing students run into an issue, they abandon the project, dismiss it completely and then move on to something, anything, else. Our middle students are the ones that will start working toward solutions in most cases. They will start to test things to "just get it done." Testing and working to see if there is a viable solution is what fail fast is all about. This is what we need more of and we need to shift the perspective to "Solutions-based thinking."

I repackage the "just get it done" into a strategy to think about how you are going to tackle the issue, work around it or abandon ship. In the references regarding fail fast, they usually call this point the pivot. If we are going to walk around the problem, that is the pivot. We turn and take a new direction at handling the project overall. There are several student phrases and their alternatives that will begin to cultivate the negative into a positive. I train this into my students all year long.

I can't do this because...	⇒	I could do this if...
This is too hard...	⇒	I am challenged by...
Can we start over?	⇒	What if we...
I think we just failed...	⇒	If I make a tweak to the instructions...

It is amazing how many adults do not have this skill. Your students will be light years ahead of the competition with just this soft skill that can change the lens in which we view issues that need solving.

The mantra of the fail fast approach is to try something, experiment a little and then pivot if it is not working. This leaves some good ideas on the cutting room floor; but they can be used again later if they are really viable solutions.

Here is what this looks like in action with the creators of Angry Birds:

> First, they had to save a company in crisis: at the beginning of 2009, Rovio was close to bankruptcy. Then, they had to create the perfect game, do every other little thing exactly right, and keep on doing it. The Heds had developed 51 titles before Angry Birds. Some of them had sold in the millions for third parties such as Namco and EA, so they decided to create their own, original intellectual property. "We thought we would need to do 10 to 15 titles until we go the right one," says 30-year-old Niklas. One afternoon in late March, in their offices overlooking a courtyard in downtown Helsinki, Jaakko Iisalo, a games designer who has been at Rovio since 2006, showed them a screenshot. He had pitched hundreds in the two months before. This one showed a cartoon flock of round birds, trudging along the ground, moving towards a pile of colorful blocks. They looked cross. "People saw this picture and it was just magical," says Niklas. Eight months and thousands of changes later, after nearly abandoning the project, Niklas watched his mother burn a Christmas turkey, distracted by playing the finished game. "She doesn't play any games. I realized: this is it." (Madrigal, 2011)

Flipped Learning Resources for Teaching Coding Courses

Software for Tutorial Video Creation

There are scores of software available for recording your lessons. The list below is by no means a comprehensive list, but it is enough to get you started.

Jing

www.techsmith.com/jing

Jing is free screencast software that allows you to create small video tutorials. It has limitations because it has newer siblings that have a cost associated with them. This one allows you to get a taste of what the other products have to offer, but leaves you craving more.

Camtasia

www.techsmith.com/Camtasia

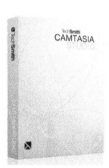

Camtasia is screencast software that gives you tools you need to customize and edit your videos. This is my recommended software. It allows you to record your screen, edit the recordings and add camera video (synchronously). The editing software reminds me of a simplified version of iMovie. The cost is $99.00 per license. There are license discounts for group purchasing if a group of teachers or your IT department purchase for you.

Screencast-o-matic

www.screencast-o-matic.com

This is a web-based tool that can record both your webcam and your screen at the same time. The free version of this account allows you to record up to 15-minute time limit, but that is perfect for flipped lessons. This service also has a paid subscription that will remove the watermark. The watermark is non-intrusive, but is visible to viewers. It is simple to use and can be setup to directly upload to your YouTube account.

Google Hangouts

http://www.google.com/+/learnmore/hangouts/

After you create your YouTube channel, you can record directly to YouTube via a Google Hangout. This will broadcast your screen or your video. You may switch between the two as you do the video. Another strategy would be to connect in a colleague or a guest speaker (up to 10 live participants) to the hangout. Once you are done with the hangout, YouTube automatically processes the video and places it on your YouTube channel. All you have to do is harvest the link and place it in your Learning Management System.

QuickTime

For Mac users, QuickTime has a screen capture feature which allows you to record longer segments than some of the free versions. The screen capture feature will record what you are doing on your computer and allow you to narrate it simultaneously. It will then export the file as a QuickTime movie file that can be uploaded to your video channel on YouTube or any other system you choose. Unfortunately, Windows users do not have this same feature.

Screencastify
https://www.screencastify.com

Screencastify is a solution that many have been looking for that will work with Chromebooks. This is an extension for Chrome that does not require any installation of a program. This has been a limitation of Chromebooks and Chromeboxes with regard to creating video tutorials in 1:1 Chrome environments.

Screencastify is a simple video screen capture software for Chrome. Just press record and the content of your tab, webcam or desktop is recorded. Easily create screencasts for video tutorials, record presentations etc. Screencastify does not depend on any plugins (like Java, Flash or others), so runs on all platforms that run Chrome (Linux, Windows, OS X) or ChromeOS (Chromebooks and Chromeboxes).

Tutorial Video Format
The video format is very simple and outlined in an even simpler graphic below:

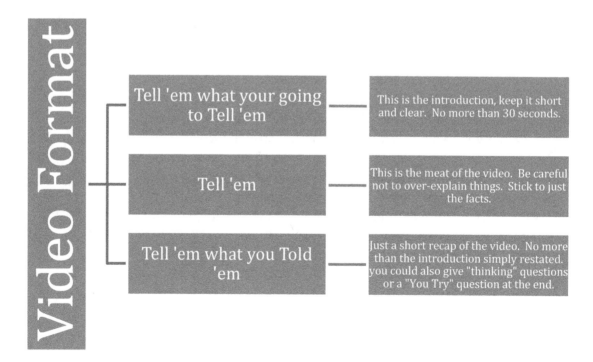

Laws of Video Creation

Being new to the basics of video production does not require us to evoke our inner Stephen Spielberg, Spike Lee, Martin Scorsese, George Lucas, Cecil B. DeMille or the Alfred Hitchcock (depending on what you are teaching). With today's high-tech cameras, the camera will do most of the work for you. However, there are some very basic tips that will have high impact in your productions.

1. Keep it short

Only shoot your video to cover one topic at a time. The goal should be no more than 15 minutes at the high end. The ideal time maximum is 10 minutes. The general rule of thumb is 1.5 minutes per grade level.

Who are your students? Many of them can't make it a whole song without fast-forwarding to the next...same with your videos. Keep them bite-sized. The students are used to the short segments found on YouTube and that is about their attention span.

2. Be Animated

Teach as you would with a room full of students. They are still there, just not at the moment. Use inflection, talk with your hands, do what is natural. Remember that you are doing this in an unnatural environment, but it will be natural to the students when they watch.

If you are acting unnatural, they will sense it and it will affect the overall quality of the video.

QUICK TIP: Stand-up when shooting the video. This will add to your animation.

Remember to use eye-contact. The lens is your eye. Look directly into the lens when you are talking to the students. It is okay to look around at different things, but make sure you continue back to make eye contact.

> **EXPERIENTIAL VOICE**
>
> I once took a distance-learning course back in the day before the Internet. The *telecourse* consisted of videos you checked out from the library. It was roughly 36 hours of a Philosophy professor standing at a podium and reading the course text. BORING didn't even describe it!

3. Work with A Partner

Working with a partner allows your tone to be more conversational. This partner can be a guest speaker with knowledge of the subject. They can be somebody that may be separated by distance, but connected via Google Hangouts. A colleague may also play the role of student while you play the role of teacher, or vice versa.

4. Add Humor

Start with a joke or funny story. Create a signature for your videos. I used to make my videos at home. Pets may walk by in the background or my kids would pass through the background. The students enjoyed the variance. Eventually, they noticed that I rarely made my videos in the same room. I overheard them discussing the different rooms in my house one day. Then, I purposely tried to find different places to make the videos (including in my car; parked in the garage). It became a game for them and enticed them to watch the videos.

5. Sound

While the camera or computer has a built-in microphone, you must be careful to eliminate as much of the ambient noise as possible. The problem with ambient noise is that we get very used to hearing it that we tune it out. Try this...sit in your area where you are going to be filming your segments. Sit very still and try to identify every sound you hear. Decide if this sound will be distracting to your video.

Record a sample video and then watch it back and try to identify if that sound is overpowering your sound.

> **EXPERIENTIAL VOICE**
>
> I once filmed an entire lesson in my classroom and, while you could hear me, I was being drowned out a lot of the time by the fans in the server closet in my room. The problem was that I was so used to hearing them, that I didn't notice them until I watched the video back.

ere is an off camera noise, you will never publish any of your videos. This is pecially true if you are filming them in school. There is always sound in a hool. You just don't want the sound to be too distracting.

6. Don't Waste Your Students Time

While you may start out with a story or a joke or something topical, remember, you are shooting for 10 minutes or less. Stay on topic. Talk about the football game when you are meeting with the students in class for a short time. Remember, they are coming to you outside of class in the videos and they are using their own time...respect it.

7. Add Callouts/Annotations

Using editing software (when you get better) you will find that adding in text when a large topic or definition comes up will help your students refocus on the topic. It gives them additional processing of not only the verbal, but reading as well. It is important to add these in for your students to see a diagram, text or other visual element other than you for a few moments just as you do with a presentation in a live lecture.

8. Video Clips

Bring the outside world to your students. Bring your camera along on events that will be topical for our students to experience. You might film something from a National Park that would be useful to your class. You may use small video clips from movie trailers to enhance the lesson on hyperbole.

9. Picture-In-Picture (PIP)

Using your image in the video personalizes the video for your students. My students reported that only hearing my voice was not enough. They wanted to see my facial expressions and gestures. They reported that it made the material more relatable. This feedback was elicited after a series of videos where I could not be seen. It was nice to know they missed me.

10. Watch your Copyrights

You will be posting your videos online. Therefore, your content will be made public. Make sure that music, graphics and all content is copyright free or you have permission. There are certain rights under "fair use" for teaching, scholarship and research. However, it is not clearly defined by amount of material or type of material. It is suggested that when in doubt...leave it out.

11. Interactive Buttons

Some of the newer software is allowing for interactive buttons. The buttons allow you to ask questions, or require user input to advance the video. This will only serve to engage the student further and entice them to watch the videos. This is a newer feature and it availability varies within different software packages.

12. Lighting

Choose a location in a well-lit area. Keep the light in front of the subject, not behind the subject (See Figure 3 and 4). Use a natural light source if possible.

Try not to rely on only the overhead fluorescent fixtures as they will cast shadows down the subject's face. This gives the appearance of being drawn out. Use a lamp with a bright bulb and a bright shade set just outside the shot a little in front of the subject and to the side. This will eliminate those shadows.

Figure 3 Natural light behind the subject allows us to see facial features.

Figure 4- Light source behind subject causes loss of facial features.

13. Mix it Up

These students are visual learners. They not only learn from what you are saying and doing, but from where you are and who you are within your videos. Liven it up and throw them a curve ball every once in a while. Here are some ideas:

- Have a taped interview or discussion panel with local experts.
- Change the location of your video to your home, office, car, or a relevant place for the topic.
- Use this as an experience to engage other colleagues and show them the benefits of flipping.
- Have an expert explain the lesson.
- Host a video conference in real time with students and an expert, tape it and have it available for those that couldn't attend.
- Start with a joke, or story.
- End with an extra credit question, a discussion topic or a brainteaser.

Flipped Learning Application

Flipped Learning Environments are great for the teaching of code! The concept of the flipped learning environment is summarized by the time in which we deliver content and the time in which students apply content. Students can choose to receive content at the moment in which they are trying to apply it to their project, learning, hands-on activity, etc. We want to free our time for problem solving and assisting the students with logic issues and metacognition. Let the direct instruction reside in a place for reference (so you don't have to keep answering the same question over and over again!

Liberate Your Time

In the simplest terms, we take the old ways of teaching and flip them. This means that students will receive direct instruction or lecture outside of class and will work on homework and practice in class with more instructor support. Thus, the term, flipped.

Educators have been doing this for quite some time in literature courses where the reading is completed outside of class and the students work through the text in class with the instructor's assistance. They may be discussing plot, theme, archetypes, etc.

When we look at a schedule for a flipped classroom and compare it to a traditional classroom, we see the differences immediately. The illustration below is a sample lesson plan from both a flipped lesson and a traditional lesson on the same topic.

Traditional Classroom	
Activity	Time
Warm-up/Bell Ringer	5 min.
Go over previous night's homework	20 min.
Lecture New Content	30 min.
Guided and independent practice and/or lab activity	5 min.
HOMEWORK: Complete independent practice.	40 min.

Flipped Classroom	
Activity	Time
Warm-up/Bell Ringer	5 min.
Q&A Time on video	10 min.
Guided and independent practice and/or lab activity	45 min.
HOMEWORK: Watch New Content Video	10 min.

Notice that the guided and independent work time is expanded in the flipped model. You now have time to do all those fun projects! Students can engage in collaborative labs, projects, problem-based learning activities that were otherwise time prohibitive.

How can a new content presentation go from 30 minutes to 10 minutes? First, there are no interruptions to go to the bathroom, behavior, requests to repeat, or slow down. Those will afford you about 10 minutes of lecture. Also, there is no discussion component. That takes place the next day with leading and probing questions in the discussion time that would otherwise be used to go over homework. Homework does not need to be reviewed because it was done in class with assistance. Time is LIBERATED!

Glossary of Terms

Algorithm	An algorithm is a set of steps or rules to follow to solve a particular problem.
Argument	A variable passed as a value to a function
Array	Also called a list. A data structure that holds a collection of values in a particular order
Boolean	A boolean is a true or false value.
Break Down (Decompose)	Breaking down (decomposing) your code is splitting it into more functions.
Bug	A bug is a problem in your code.
Call a Function	Calling a function actually gives the command, so the computer will run the code for that function.
Canvas	The screen in which our graphics programs are drawn.
Code	Code is the name for the instructions you write to a computer in a program.
Command	A command is an instruction you can give to Karel.
Comment	A message in your code that explains what is going on.
Comment Out	Commenting out code makes the computer ignore it, so it does not run.
Comparison operator	Used to make comparisons between values.
Computer	A person or device that makes calculations, stores data, and executes instructions according to a program.
Computing	Executing instructions, calculating, or using a computer.
Condition	A condition is code that you put inside an if statement or while-loop.
Console	A computer program that is run using a text-only interface.
Constant	A variable in a program that has a value that does not change.
Control Structure	A control structure lets us change the flow of the code.
Coordinate system	A coordinate system uses numbers as coordinates to place objects in a geometric space.
Counter	A variable used to count the number of times an action has been performed
Curly Bracket	An open curly bracket is { and a close curly bracket is }
Debugging	Debugging is fixing a problem in your code.

Declare a Variable	Declaring a variable is defining it for the first time.
Decomposition	Decomposition is breaking your program into smaller parts.
Decrement	To subtract from or decrease
Define a Function	Defining a function means to teach the computer a new command and explain what it should do when receiving that command.
Degrees	A unit of measurement of angles
DRY Principle	Don't repeat yourself: try to simplify your code and avoid repeating code unnecessarily.
Edge Case	An edge case is a problem in your code that only occurs in extreme situations.
Event	An event is an action (such as clicking the mouse or pressing a key on the keyboard) that a program detects and uses as input.
Fencepost Problem	A problem when using a while loop where you forget one action at the beginning or the end.
For Loop	A for loop lets us repeat code a fixed number of times.
Function	A function is a way to teach Karel a new word.
Function body	The part of a function that contains the commands
Global variable	A variable that can be used throughout a program, in every scope
Grid	A two-dimensional array
HTML	Hypertext Markup Language
HTML Documentation	Documentation and syntax for HTML
HTML Tag	Tags are the building blocks of an HTML document
If Else Statement	Control structure that lets us do either one section of code or another depending on a test.
If Statement	An if statement lets you ask a question to the program and only run code if the answer is true.
Increment	To add to or increase
Indentation	Indentation is the visual structure of how your code is laid out. It uses tabs to organize code into a hierarchy.
Integer	A whole number (not a fraction)
Iterate	A single run through the instructions contained a loop
JavaScript Documentation	Documentation for the syntax and objects in Javascript that we use on CodeHS.
List	Also called an array. A data structure that holds a collection of values in a particular order
Local variable	A variable that is restricted to use in a certain scope of a program
Logical operator	Used to make logical associations between boolean values
Loop	A loop is a way to repeat code in your program.

Loop-and-a-half	A loop, most often set with while(true), that has a break in the loop body.
lowerCamelCase	lowerCamelCase is a naming convention where the first letter is lower case, and each subsequent start of a word is upper case.
Magic Number	A number in your code that appears arbitrary. These should all be replaced with calculations or constants.
Nested for loop	A for loop written, or "nested", inside of another for loop.
Nested Function	A nested function is a function that is defined inside another function. This should be avoided.
Object	Also called a dictionary or map. Lets us store pairs of keys that are matched with a specific value.
Parameter	A variable passed in from outside the function
Parentheses	(and)
Pop	To remove the item in the last position from an array
Postcondition	What should be true after the function is called
Precondition	Assumptions we make about what must be true before the function is called.
Programming Style	The way your code is written is the style. It covers the aspects of the code that goes beyond whether or not it just works.
Pseudocode	Pseudocode is a brief explanation of code in plain English.
Push	To add an item to a list or array
Randomize	To generate or select a random object
Read Like a Story	Programs that "Read like a story" have good decomposition and make the code easy to follow.
readFloat	Allows for the reading of user input when a float number is used
readInt	Allows for the reading of user input when an integer is used
readLine	Allows for the reading of user input when a string is used
Return	Exit a function and return a value
Runtime error	An error that results in a crash when the program is run.
Scope	In what part of the program the variable exits
Semicolon	A punctuation marks that looks like ;
Sentinel	A constant that has the specific purpose of being the value that breaks out of a loop.
Set	A data structure that stores values in no particular order. Each value can only appear once in the set.
Start Function	This is the function that is called when you click run.
String	A sequence of characters
Syntax error	An error in the sequence of words or rules in a program that prevents the program from running.
Timer	Timers are used to used perform repeated action in a program
Top Down Design	Top down design is a method for breaking our program down into smaller parts.

Variable	A symbol or container that holds a value.
While Loop	Lets us repeat code as long as something is true.

References

About Us. (n.d.). Retrieved January 29, 2016, from https://code.org/about

Dann, W., Slater, D., Paoletti, L., Cosgrove, D., Culyba, D., & Tang, P. (2014, September). *Alice 3: How-to guide (part 1 - getting started)* [PDF].

Hopper, G. M. (1952). The education of a computer. *Proceedings of the 1952 ACM National Meeting (Pittsburg) (ACM '52),* 243-249. Retrieved January 25, 2016.

Linney, T. (2015, July 06). Coding in the Common Core. Retrieved January 25, 2016, from http://www.edutopia.org/blog/coding-in-the-common-core-tara-linney

Madrigal, A. C. (2011, March 09). How Rovio Fought Off Bankruptcy to Make Angry Birds. Retrieved January 22, 2018, from https://www.theatlantic.com/technology/archive/2011/03/how-rovio-fought-off-bankruptcy-to-make-angry-birds/72250/

McKay, E. N. (2013). *UI is communication: How to design intuitive, user centered interfaces by focusing on effective communication.* Waltham, MA: Elsevier.

Petty, K. (n.d.). The Tech Classroom. Retrieved May 03, 2016, from http://www.thetechclassroom.com

Programming. (n.d.). Retrieved January 25, 2016, from http://www.urbandictionary.com/define.php?term=Programming

Project Based Teaching Rubric. (2015). Retrieved October 19, 2016, from

http://www.bie.org/object/document/project_based_teaching_rubric#

Project Design Rubric. (2015). Retrieved October 18, 2016, from

http://www.bie.org/object/document/project_design_rubric#

Protocol and materials guide to the screen education process [Scholarly project].

(2006). In *American Film Institute*. Retrieved January 28, 2016, from

http://www.unitedstreaming.com/videos/42845/D2B15956-1279-3B00-

CD01B9EA8FD93498.pdf

Read the Standards. (n.d.). Retrieved January 26, 2016, from

http://www.corestandards.org/read-the-standards/

Resnick, M., Maloney, J., Monroy-Hernández, A., Rusk, N., Eastmond, E.,

Brennan, K., . . . Kafai, Y. (2009). Scratch: Programming for all.

Communications of the ACM, 52(11), 60-67.

Scratch - About. (n.d.). Retrieved January 28, 2016, from

https://scratch.mit.edu/about/

The History of Computer Programming. (n.d.). Retrieved January 25, 2016, from

http://visual.ly/history-computer-programming

What is Alice? (n.d.). Retrieved January 28, 2016, from

http://www.alice.org/index.php?page=what_is_alice/what_is_alice

Wilson, K. (n.d.). How to start integrating coding into project-based learning.

Retrieved January 31, 2016, from http://edtechteacher.org/how-to-start-

integrating-coding-into-project-based-learning-from-kate-wilson/

Post-Reading Self-Assessment

DIRECTIONS: Please fill out the following self-assessment at the close of the workshop. Be honest, don't over-interpret questions...go with your gut!

Rate your current understanding of coding after today's workshop.
   a) I have a better understanding than I came in with today and feel somewhat confident bringing this back to the students.
   b) I learned a few things today and I am charged up to go back and share this with my other colleagues and my students.
   c) I am leaving more confused than ever...I think I needed a beginner class.
   d) I am leaving wishing there were less beginners in the room. I feel that it held the presenter back.

List any questions that you might have after reading this book. Email them to me at kevin@kevinmsteele.com. I would love your feedback.

Now, what is your understanding of coding or code?

What are three things you are going to do when you implement coding with your classes?

What is your coding class vision at the end of the book?

www.ingramcontent.com/pod-product-compliance
Lightning Source LLC
LaVergne TN
LVHW081700050326
832903LV00026B/1849